Vanessa-Ann's
Holidays In Cross-Stitch

1992

Vanessa-Ann's
Holidays In
Cross-Stitch
1992

To Ryne, from all my hearts:

friend, colleague, accomplice.

I love you,
Jo

Library of Congress Catalog Number: 86-62285
ISBN: 0-8487-1037-1
ISSN: 0890-8230
Manufactured in the United States of America
First Printing 1991

Executive Editor: Nancy Janice Fitzpatrick
Director of Manufacturing: Jerry Higdon
Art Director: James Boone
Copy Chief: Mary Jean Haddin

Holidays In Cross-Stitch 1992

Editor: Laurie Pate Sewell
Editorial Assistant: Shannon Leigh Sexton
Assistant Copy Editor: Susan Smith Cheatham
Production Manager: Rick Litton
Associate Production Manager: Theresa L. Beste
Production Assistant: Pam Beasley Bullock
Designer: Diana Smith Morrison
Computer Artist: Karen Tindall Tillery
Artist: Eleanor Cameron
Photographers: Ryne Hazen, Mikel Covey

The Vanessa-Ann Collection offers heartfelt thanks to Mary Gaskill at Trends and Traditions of Ogden, Utah; to Anita Louise at Bearlace Cottage in Park City, Utah; and to The Lion House in Salt Lake City, Utah, for allowing us to photograph on their premises. We sincerely appreciate their trust and cooperation.

The Vanessa-Ann Collection Staff

Designers

1992
Contents

Introduction

Welcome a new year with a multitude of new and exciting designs from The Vanessa-Ann Collection. *Holidays in Cross-Stitch 1992* celebrates traditional holidays and introduces others that are not as well known. And this year, of course, we are commemorating the 500th anniversary of Christopher Columbus's discovery of America. Also unique to this year's book is a beautiful floral afghan featuring a special flower for each month. So choose some of your favorites and start stitching now. We at Vanessa-Ann hope you will enjoy another year stitched full of beauty and color, richness and warmth.

For Mom

1992

JANUARY
S	M	T	W	T	F	S
			1	2	3	4
5	6	7	8	9	10	11
12	13	14	15	16	17	18
19	20	21	22	23	24	25
26	27	28	29	30	31	

FEBRUARY
S	M	T	W	T	F	S
						1
2	3	4	5	6	7	8
9	10	11	12	13	14	15
16	17	18	19	20	21	22
23	24	25	26	27	28	29

MARCH
S	M	T	W	T	F	S
1	2	3	4	5	6	7
8	9	10	11	12	13	14
15	16	17	18	19	20	21
22	23	24	25	26	27	28
29	30	31				

APRIL
S	M	T	W	T	F	S
			1	2	3	4
5	6	7	8	9	10	11
12	13	14	15	16	17	18
19	20	21	22	23	24	25
26	27	28	29	30		

MAY
S	M	T	W	T	F	S
					1	2
3	4	5	6	7	8	9
10	11	12	13	14	15	16
17	18	19	20	21	22	23
24	25	26	27	28	29	30
31						

JUNE
S	M	T	W	T	F	S
	1	2	3	4	5	6
7	8	9	10	11	12	13
14	15	16	17	18	19	20
21	22	23	24	25	26	27
28	29	30				

JULY
S	M	T	W	T	F	S
			1	2	3	4
5	6	7	8	9	10	11
12	13	14	15	16	17	18
19	20	21	22	23	24	25
26	27	28	29	30	31	

AUGUST
S	M	T	W	T	F	S
						1
2	3	4	5	6	7	8
9	10	11	12	13	14	15
16	17	18	19	20	21	22
23	24	25	26	27	28	29
30	31					

SEPTEMBER
S	M	T	W	T	F	S
		1	2	3	4	5
6	7	8	9	10	11	12
13	14	15	16	17	18	19
20	21	22	23	24	25	26
27	28	29	30			

OCTOBER
S	M	T	W	T	F	S
				1	2	3
4	5	6	7	8	9	10
11	12	13	14	15	16	17
18	19	20	21	22	23	24
25	26	27	28	29	30	31

NOVEMBER
S	M	T	W	T	F	S
1	2	3	4	5	6	7
8	9	10	11	12	13	14
15	16	17	18	19	20	21
22	23	24	25	26	27	28
29	30					

DECEMBER
S	M	T	W	T	F	S
		1	2	3	4	5
6	7	8	9	10	11	12
13	14	15	16	17	18	19
20	21	22	23	24	25	26
27	28	29	30	31		

ALL YEAR
Flower·of· the·Month Afghan

Stroll through a sun-drenched garden, imagine the sweet aroma of fresh flowers in bloom, and celebrate the seasons with our flower-of-the-month afghan. Stitched on Vanessa-Ann Afghan Weave, this floral creation features twelve beautiful designs—one for each month. So, whether the air is warm or frosty, you can enjoy your own special flower garden all year long.

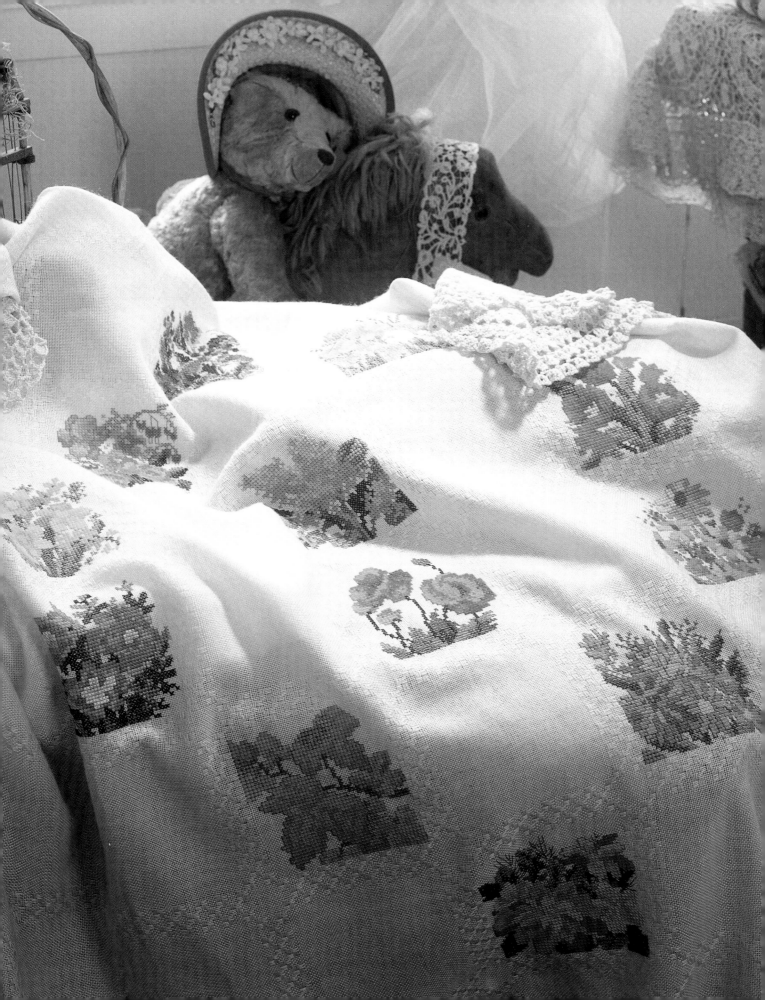

Crochet Trim

MATERIALS

DMC Brilliant Crochet Cotton
(Size 10): 6 (218-yard) balls
Ecru

Size 7 steel crochet hook (or size
to obtain gauge)

DIRECTIONS

1. To hem afghan, turn under ¾"
twice along all raw edges, mitering
corners. Slipstitch hem in place.

2. *Gauge:* 4 V-sts = 2". Finished
edging is 3½" wide. ***Rnd 1:*** With
right side facing, join thread with a
sl st in any corner, 2 sc in same
corner, * sc evenly to next corner,
3 sc in corner, rep from * around,
end with sc in beg corner, sl st in
first sc = 461 sts across each long
edge, 381 sts across each short
edge (not including center corner
sts). ***Rnd 2:*** Ch 5 for first dc and ch
2, dc in same st, * sk 2 sc, (dc, ch 2,
dc) in next sc (V-st made), (sk 3 sc,
V-st in next sc) across to 2 sts
before next corner, sk 2 sc, V-st in
center corner st, rep from *
around, end with sl st in 3rd ch of
beg ch-5 = 115 V-sts across each
long edge, 95 V-sts across each
short edge. ***Rnd 3:*** Sl st into corner ch-2 sp, ch 4 for first dc and ch
1, 3 dc in same sp, * (ch 1, 3 dc in
next ch-2 sp) across to next corner,
(3 dc, ch 1, 3 dc) in corner ch-2 sp,
rep from * around, end with 2 dc in
beg corner, sl st in 3rd ch of beg
ch-4. ***Rnd 4:*** Sl st into ch-1 sp, ch 5
for first dc and ch 2, (dc, ch 2, dc) in
same sp, * (V-st in next ch-1 sp)
across to next corner, (dc, ch 2) 3
times in corner sp, dc in same corner sp, rep from * around, end
with (dc, ch 2) in beg corner, sl st
in 3rd ch of beg ch-5. ***Rnd 5:*** Rep
rnd 3. ***Rnd 6:*** *Note:* On this rnd
work V-st as follows: (dc, ch 1, dc).
Sl st into corner sp, ch 5 for first tr
and ch 1, (tr, ch 1) twice in same
sp, V-st in same sp, * [(V-st, ch 1,
tr, ch 1, V-st) in next sp for shell]
across to next corner, [V-st, ch 1,
(tr, ch 1) 3 times, V-st] in corner
sp, rep from * around, end with
(V-st, ch 1) in beg corner, sl st in
4th ch of beg ch-5. ***Rnd 7:*** Ch 5, sc
in 3rd tr of corner, * (ch 5, sc in
center tr of next shell) across to
next corner, ch 5, sc in first tr of
corner, ch 5, sc in 3rd tr of corner,
rep from * around, end with ch 5,
sl st in base of beg ch-5. ***Rnd 8:*** Sl
st into center ch of corner lp, ch 5
for first tr and ch 1, (tr, ch 1) 3
times in same st, tr in same st,
* [(tr, ch 1) 4 times in center ch of
next lp, tr in same st] across to
next corner lp, (tr, ch 1) 6 times in
center ch of corner lp, tr in same
st, rep from * around, end with (tr,
ch 1) twice in beg corner, sl st in
4th ch of beg ch-5. ***Rnd 9:*** Ch 5, sc
in 5th tr of corner, * (ch 5, sc in
center tr of next group) across to
next corner, ch 5, sc in 3rd tr of
corner, ch 5, sc in 5th tr of corner,
rep from * around, sl st in base of
beg ch-5. ***Rnd 10:*** Rep rnd 8. Fas-
ten off.

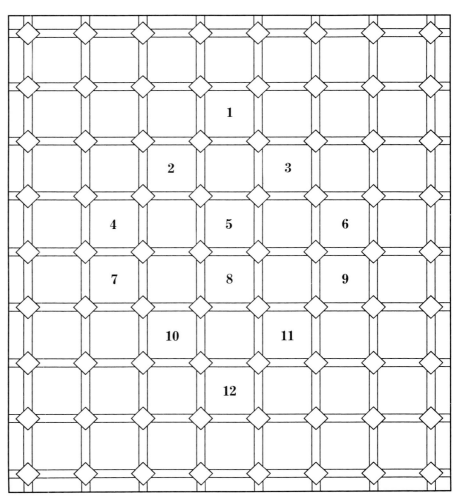

1. **January: Bearberries**
2. **February: Roses**
3. **March: Crocuses**
4. **April: Daffodils**
5. **May: Lilacs**
6. **June: Tulips**
7. **July: Wild Roses**
8. **August: Poppies**
9. **September: Black-eyed Susans**
10. **October: Leaves**
11. **November: Chrysanthemums**
12. **December: Poinsettias**

Diagram

Flower of the Month

During the time that most of nature is sleeping, the bright red berries of this evergreen shrub add color to an otherwise barren winter landscape.

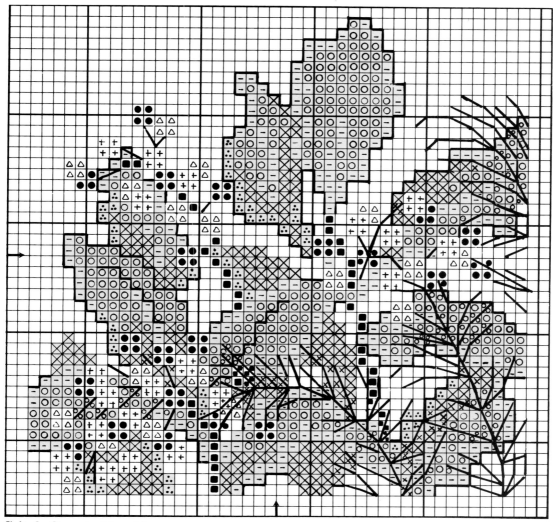

Stitch Count: 44 x 44

Afghan Square: Bearberries

SAMPLE
Stitched on Vanessa-Ann Afghan Weave 18 over 2 threads, the finished design size is 4⅞″ x 4⅞″. The fabric was cut 49″ x 59″ for complete afghan. See Suppliers for afghan material. Refer to page 10 for crochet instructions and for diagram showing placement of each design.

FABRICS
Aida 11
Aida 14
Aida 18
Hardanger 22

DESIGN SIZES
4″ x 4″
3⅛″ x 3⅛″
2½″ x 2½″
2″ x 2″

Anchor		DMC (used for sample)	
Step 1: Cross-stitch (3 strands)			
59	+	326	Rose-vy. dk.
42	△	3350	Dusty Rose-dk.
72	●	902	Garnet-vy. dk.
214	–	368	Pistachio Green-lt.
876	∴	502	Blue Green
861	○	3363	Pine Green-med.
246	✕	319	Pistachio Green-vy. dk.
914	■	3772	Pecan-med.

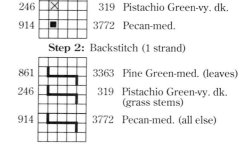

Step 2: Backstitch (1 strand)

861		3363	Pine Green-med. (leaves)
246		319	Pistachio Green-vy. dk. (grass stems)
914		3772	Pecan-med. (all else)

Man-Watchers Week

It is easy to imagine a maiden a couple of centuries ago making a sampler like this for her hope chest. Stitching a sampler portraying men in their customary activities was one way to keep up her hopes as she watched and waited for the right man. Man watching is still alive and well today; a week has even been set aside for the purpose. Or you can stitch this handsome piece as a gift to show the most-watched man in *your* life how much you appreciate him.

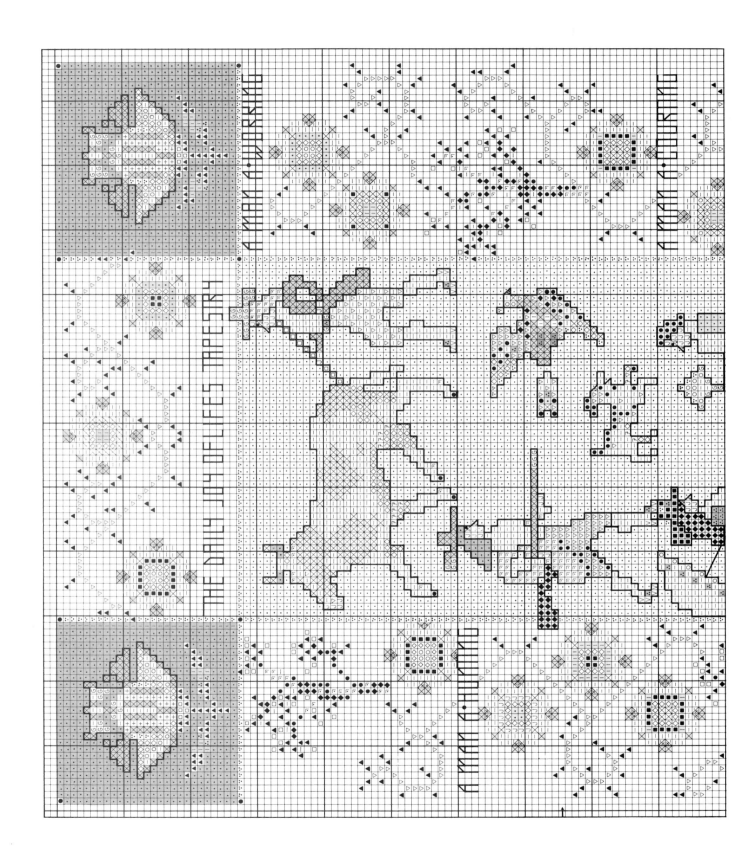

Stitch Count: 115 x 151

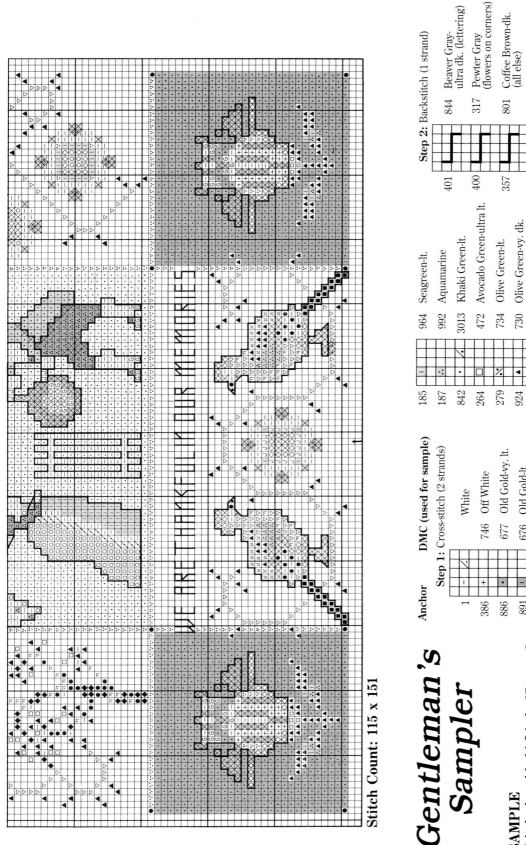

Gentleman's Sampler

SAMPLE
Stitched on khaki Linda 27 over 2 threads, the finished design size is 8⅝" x 11⅛". The fabric was cut 15" x 17".

FABRICS DESIGN SIZES
Aida 11   10½" x 13¾"
Aida 14   8¼" x 10¾"
Aida 18   6⅜" x 8⅜"
Hardanger 22 5¼" x 6⅞"

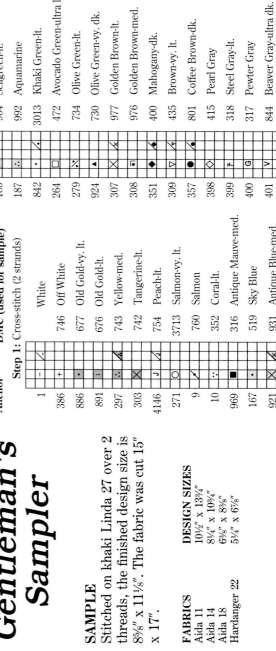

Anchor		DMC (used for sample)
	Step 1: Cross-stitch (2 strands)	
1	- /	White
386	+	746 Off White
886	•	677 Old Gold-vy. lt.
891	ı	676 Old Gold-lt.
297	⊠	743 Yellow-med.
303	J	742 Tangerine-lt.
4146	⋰	754 Peach-lt.
271	○	3713 Salmon-vy. lt.
9	◜	760 Salmon
10	∴	352 Coral-lt.
969	■	316 Antique Mauve-med.
167	•	519 Sky Blue
921	⊠	931 Antique Blue-med.
185	ı	964 Seagreen-lt.
187	∴	992 Aquamarine
842	•	3013 Khaki Green-lt.
264	▱	472 Avocado Green-ultra lt.
279	⁒	734 Olive Green-lt.
924	◀	730 Olive Green-vy. dk.
307	⊠	977 Golden Brown-lt.
308	⊡	976 Golden Brown-med.
351	◆	400 Mahogany-dk.
309	▷	435 Brown-vy. lt.
357	●	801 Coffee Brown-dk.
398	◇	415 Pearl Gray
399	F	318 Steel Gray-lt.
400	G	317 Pewter Gray
401	V	844 Beaver Gray-ultra dk.

	Step 2: Backstitch (1 strand)
401	844 Beaver Gray-ultra dk. (lettering)
400	317 Pewter Gray (flowers on corners)
357	801 Coffee Brown-dk. (all else)

	Step 3: French Knot (1 strand)
401	844 Beaver Gray-ultra dk.

FEBRUARY
Flower of the Month

The rose was the world's first cultivated flower and is considered its favorite. During the height of Greek civilization, this lovely flower was called "the queen of flowers." Known for its sweet fragrance and romantic connotation, the rose is very popular on Valentine's Day.

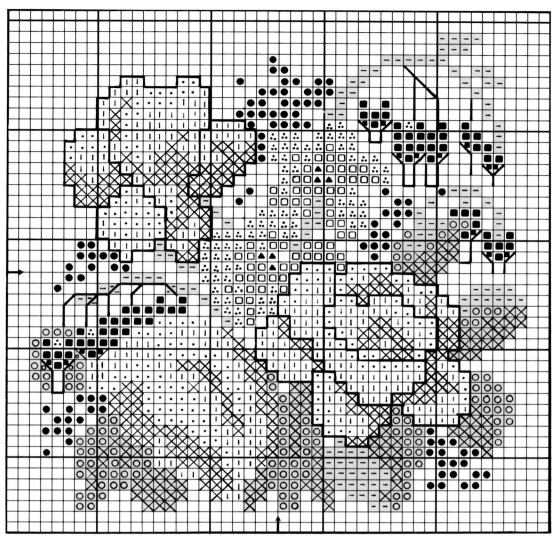

Stitch Count: 44 x 44

Afghan Square: Roses

SAMPLE

Stitched on Vanessa-Ann Afghan Weave 18 over 2 threads, the finished design size is 4⅞" x 4⅞". The fabric was cut 49" x 59" for complete afghan. See Suppliers for afghan material. Refer to page 10 for crochet instructions and for diagram showing placement of each design.

FABRICS	DESIGN SIZES
Aida 11	4" x 4"
Aida 14	3⅛" x 3⅛"
Aida 18	2½" x 2½"
Hardanger 22	2" x 2"

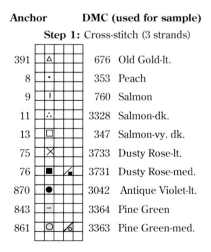

Anchor		DMC (used for sample)	
		Step 1: Cross-stitch (3 strands)	
391	△	676	Old Gold-lt.
8	·	353	Peach
9	I	760	Salmon
11	∴	3328	Salmon-dk.
13	□	347	Salmon-vy. dk.
75	✕	3733	Dusty Rose-lt.
76	■ ◢	3731	Dusty Rose-med.
870	●	3042	Antique Violet-lt.
843	–	3364	Pine Green
861	○ ◣	3363	Pine Green-med.

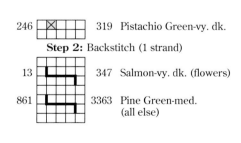

246	✕	319	Pistachio Green-vy. dk.
		Step 2: Backstitch (1 strand)	
13		347	Salmon-vy. dk. (flowers)
861		3363	Pine Green-med. (all else)

FEBRUARY 14
Valentine's Day

Valentine's Day is the perfect time to give and receive sweet greetings. These soft-sculptured hearts will convey warm sentiments on this special occasion. Each fabric heart is embellished with plastic canvas applied in various ways. Weaving pieces of canvas together, stitching through two layers, and embellishing the canvas with special stitches and beads make each heart unique.

Soft-Sculptured Hearts

SAMPLE for Green Heart
Stitched on cream Plastic Canvas 14 over 1 mesh, the finished design size is 3⅝" x 2⅛" for Section 1 and 2⅛" x 3⅝" for Section 2. Use 1 (4" x 4") sheet of plastic canvas for each section. Complete Steps 1 and 2 of color code for both sections. Cut out each section. Bold lines on graphs indicate cutting lines. Weave Sections 1 and 2 together (see Diagram A). Complete Step 3 of color code for both sections, stitching through both layers where indicated. See General Instructions for information on working with plastic canvas. See Suppliers for Plastic Canvas 14.

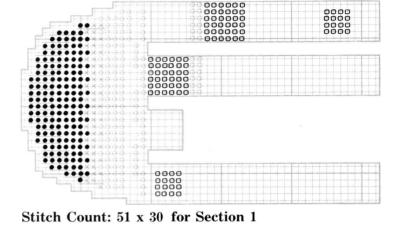

Stitch Count: 51 x 30 for Section 1

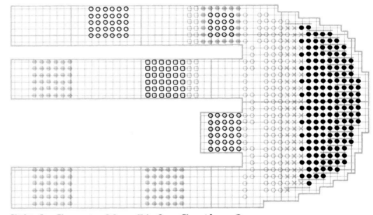

Stitch Count: 30 x 51 for Section 2

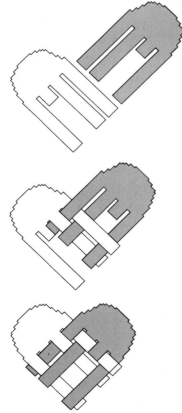

Diagram A

Anchor		DMC (used for sample)
Step 1: Cross-stitch (2 strands)		
893		224 Shell Pink-lt.
893 399		224 Shell Pink-lt. (1 strand)+ 451 Shell Gray-dk. (1 strand)
266		3347 Yellow Green-med.
399	●	451 Shell Gray-dk.
Step 2: Long Stitch (2 strands)		
399		451 Shell Gray-dk.

Step 3: Cross-stitch (2 strands)
(stitch through both layers)

Anchor		DMC
893	⊕	224 Shell Pink-lt.
266	⊞	3347 Yellow Green-med.
399		451 Shell Gray-dk.

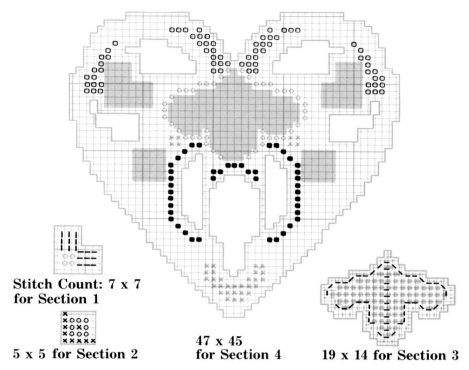

**Stitch Count: 7 x 7
for Section 1**

5 x 5 for Section 2

**47 x 45
for Section 4**

19 x 14 for Section 3

SAMPLE for Purple Heart

Stitched on cream Plastic Canvas 14 over 1 mesh, the finished design size is ½″ x ½″ for Section 1, ⅜″ x 3⅜″ for Section 2, 1⅜″ x 1″ for Section 3, and 3⅜″ x 3¼″ for Section 4. Use 1 (4″ x 4″) sheet of plastic canvas for Sections 1, 2, and 3 together and 1 (4″ x 4″) sheet for Section 4. Cut out 2 each of Sections 1 and 2 and 1 each of Sections 3 and 4, including inner sections. Bold lines on graphs indicate cutting lines. Position Section 1s, 2s, and 3 on 4, matching shapes to gray areas shown on graph. Complete stitching of all sections, stitching through both layers where necessary. See General Instructions for information on working with plastic canvas. See Suppliers for Plastic Canvas 14.

Anchor		DMC	(used for sample)
Step 1: Cross-stitch (2 strands)			
1	⊙		White (stitch through both layers)
8		761	Salmon-lt.
119		333	Blue Violet-dk. (stitch through both layers)
128	×	800	Delft-pale
128	✕	800	Delft-pale (stitch through both layers)
269	■	936	Avocado Green-vy. dk.
882	⊡	407	Pecan
882	⊡	407	Pecan (stitch through both layers)
Step 2: Backstitch (2 strands)			
1			White (stitch through both layers)
128		800	Delft-pale (stitch through both layers)
Step 3: Cut and Overcast (2 strands)			
882		407	Pecan

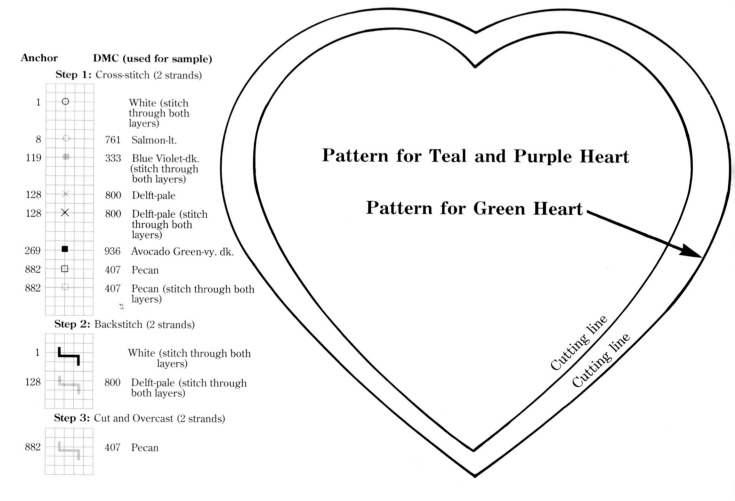

Pattern for Teal and Purple Heart

Pattern for Green Heart

Cutting line

Cutting line

22

SAMPLE for Teal Heart

Stitched on cream Plastic Canvas 14 over 1 mesh, the finished design size is 3⅜″ x 3¼″. Use 1 (4″ x 4″) sheet of plastic canvas. Complete Step 1 of color code. Cut out design, including inner rectangle. Bold lines on graph indicate cutting lines. Complete Step 2 of color code (see Diagrams B and C). Complete remaining stitching according to color code. See General Instructions for information on working with plastic canvas. See Suppliers for Plastic Canvas 14.

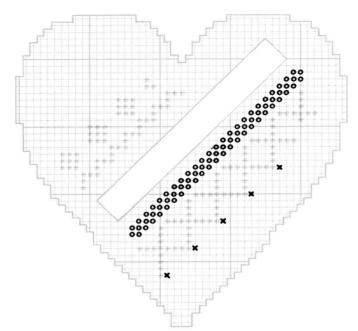

Stitch Count: 47 x 45

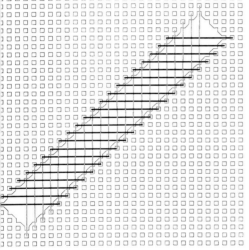

Diagram B

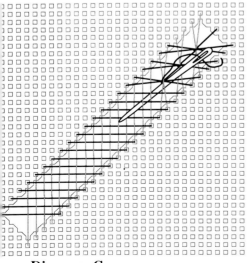

Diagram C

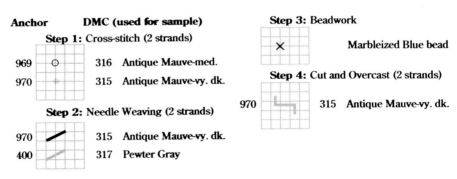

Anchor		DMC (used for sample)
Step 1: Cross-stitch (2 strands)		
969	⊙	316 Antique Mauve-med.
970	+	315 Antique Mauve-vy. dk.
Step 2: Needle Weaving (2 strands)		
970	╱	315 Antique Mauve-vy. dk.
400	╱	317 Pewter Gray

Step 3: Beadwork		
✕		Marbleized Blue bead
Step 4: Cut and Overcast (2 strands)		
970		315 Antique Mauve-vy. dk.

MATERIALS (for 1)

Completed cross-stitch on cream Plastic Canvas 14
1 (10″-square) piece of green, teal, or purple fabric; matching thread
Cream thread
¾ yard (⅜″-wide) cream ribbon
Stuffing

DIRECTIONS

The patterns include ¼″ seam allowances.

1. Using pattern, cut 2 hearts from fabric.

2. With rights sides facing and raw edges aligned, stitch front to back, leaving an opening for turning. Turn. Stuff moderately. Slip-stitch opening closed.

3. Using thread, center and tack design piece to front of heart.

4. For hanger, cut 1 (14″) length of ribbon and fold in half. Tack fold to top center of heart. Tie ribbon in a knot to cover stitches. Then knot ends of ribbon together to make a loop.

5. To complete heart, make a 4-loop bow from 10½″ of ribbon. Stitch bow to top center of heart front.

MARCH
Flower of the Month

Even if you don't have a green thumb, you will certainly have success with crocuses. Once planted, nature takes charge, and they divide to spread themselves. The most popular are the purple and those called "cloth-of-gold," a bright orange-yellow.

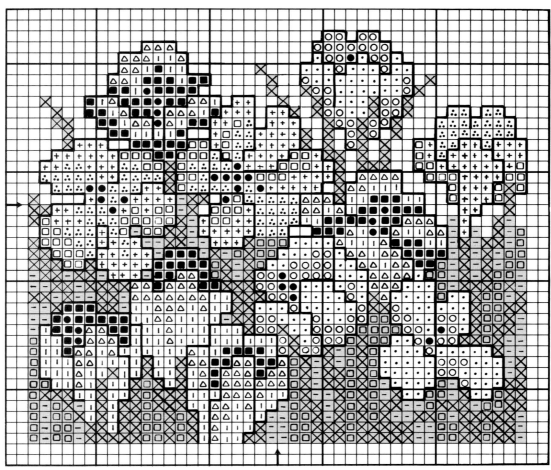

Stitch Count: 44 x 38

Afghan Square: Crocuses

SAMPLE

Stitched on Vanessa-Ann Afghan Weave 18 over 2 threads, the finished design size is 4⅞″ x 4¼″. The fabric was cut 49″ x 59″ for complete afghan. See Suppliers for afghan material. Refer to page 10 for crochet instructions and for diagram showing placement of each design.

FABRICS	DESIGN SIZES
Aida 11	4″ x 3½″
Aida 14	3⅛″ x 2¾″
Aida 18	2½″ x 2⅛″
Hardanger 22	2″ x 1¾″

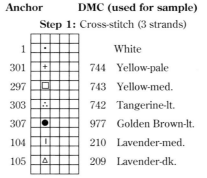

Anchor		DMC (used for sample)	
Step 1: Cross-stitch (3 strands)			
1	·		White
301	+	744	Yellow-pale
297	□	743	Yellow-med.
303	∴	742	Tangerine-lt.
307	●	977	Golden Brown-lt.
104	I	210	Lavender-med.
105	△	209	Lavender-dk.

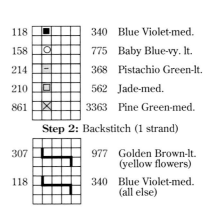

Anchor		DMC	
118	■	340	Blue Violet-med.
158	○	775	Baby Blue-vy. lt.
214	-	368	Pistachio Green-lt.
210	□	562	Jade-med.
861	✕	3363	Pine Green-med.

Step 2: Backstitch (1 strand)			
307		977	Golden Brown-lt. (yellow flowers)
118		340	Blue Violet-med. (all else)

MARCH 25
Pecan Day

This day marks the anniversary of the planting of pecan trees by George Washington at Mount Vernon in 1775. Native to southern North America, the trees were a gift from fellow Virginian Thomas Jefferson, who had planted several at Monticello. Some of those trees still stand today, which is a fine tribute to the trees bearing what is sometimes called "America's own nut."

Stitch Count: 69 x 91

Pecan Day Sampler

SAMPLE
Stitched on Rustico 14 over 1 thread, the finished design size is 4⅞″ x 6½″. The fabric was cut 11″ x 13″. To complete project, wrap design around a padded base and mount on an antique box.

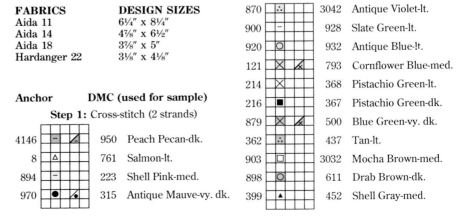

FABRICS	DESIGN SIZES
Aida 11	6¼″ x 8¼″
Aida 14	4⅞″ x 6½″
Aida 18	3⅞″ x 5″
Hardanger 22	3⅛″ x 4⅛″

Anchor — **DMC (used for sample)**

Step 1: Cross-stitch (2 strands)

Anchor		DMC	
4146		950	Peach Pecan-dk.
8		761	Salmon-lt.
894		223	Shell Pink-med.
970		315	Antique Mauve-vy. dk.
870		3042	Antique Violet-lt.
900		928	Slate Green-lt.
920		932	Antique Blue-lt.
121		793	Cornflower Blue-med.
214		368	Pistachio Green-lt.
216		367	Pistachio Green-dk.
879		500	Blue Green-vy. dk.
362		437	Tan-lt.
903		3032	Mocha Brown-med.
898		611	Drab Brown-dk.
399		452	Shell Gray-med.

APRIL
Flower of the Month

We know, without a doubt, that spring is here when the daffodils begin to bloom. Their bright splash of color brings the whole garden back to life after the long, cold winter.

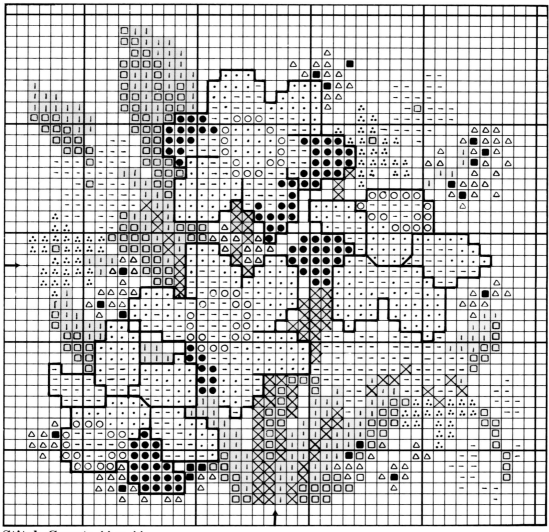

Stitch Count: 44 x 44

Afghan Square: Daffodils

SAMPLE
Stitched on Vanessa-Ann Afghan Weave 18 over 2 threads, the finished design size is 4⅞″ x 4⅞″. The fabric was cut 49″ x 59″ for complete afghan. See Suppliers for afghan material. Refer to page 10 for crochet instructions and for diagram showing placement of each design.

FABRICS
Aida 11
Aida 14
Aida 18
Hardanger 22

DESIGN SIZES
4″ x 4″
3⅛″ x 3⅛″
2½″ x 2½″
2″ x 2″

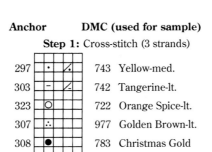

Anchor			DMC (used for sample)	
Step 1: Cross-stitch (3 strands)				
297	•	⁄	743	Yellow-med.
303	−	⁄	742	Tangerine-lt.
323	O		722	Orange Spice-lt.
307	∴		977	Golden Brown-lt.
308	●		783	Christmas Gold

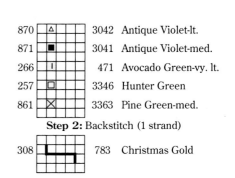

		DMC	
870	△	3042	Antique Violet-lt.
871	■	3041	Antique Violet-med.
266	I	471	Avocado Green-vy. lt.
257	□	3346	Hunter Green
861	✕	3363	Pine Green-med.

Step 2: Backstitch (1 strand)

			DMC	
308		L	783	Christmas Gold

A P R I L 4 – 5
Spring Arts Festival

Every April, the folks in Gainesville, Florida, set aside two days in honor of the arrival of spring to celebrate with artisans from across the country. Craftspeople gather to exhibit their winter's work and to enjoy the handiwork of others at the Spring Arts Festival. Celebrate the beauty of spring yourself, not just for two days, but each day throughout the year, with this delightful sponge-painted table topped with a colorful cross-stitch design.

31

Floral Table

SAMPLE

Stitched on ivory Linda 27 over 2 threads, the finished design size is 9⅜" x 9⅜". The fabric was cut 16" x 16". See Suppliers for Shaker table.

The table was first painted with white latex and then, using a natural sponge, was sponge-painted with pink and light blue acrylic paints. Sponge-paint as desired by applying a small amount of 1 color to dry sponge and dabbing paint randomly on wood. Let dry. Repeat with remaining color.

To attach design piece to table-top inset, zigzag edges of needle-work. Cut 1 piece of fleece same size as inset. Glue to inset. Center and wrap design piece around padded inset, gluing edges to back. Glue 50" length of ¼" silver cording around edges of mounted design piece. To assemble table, follow manufacturer's instructions.

FABRICS	DESIGN SIZES
Aida 11	11½" x 11½"
Aida 14	9⅛" x 9⅛"
Aida 18	7" x 7"
Hardanger 22	5¾" x 5¾"

Anchor		DMC	(used for sample)

Step 1: Cross-stitch (2 strands)

Anchor		DMC	
366	+	951	Peach Pecan-lt.
881	∴	945	Peach Beige
4146	△	950	Peach Pecan-dk.
893	⊠	224	Shell Pink-lt.
849	▲	927	Slate Green-med.
117	▪	341	Blue Violet-lt.
121	–	794	Cornflower Blue-lt.
940	○	793	Cornflower Blue-med.
130	∴	799	Delft-med.
131	⊠	798	Delft-dk.
860	–	3053	Green Gray
860	◯	3053	Green Gray (1 strand)
859	·	3052	Green Gray-med.
846	∴	3051	Green Gray-dk.
862	⊠	935	Avocado Green-dk.
388	ǀ	3033	Mocha Brown-vy. lt.
882	■	407	Pecan
936	●	632	Pecan-dk.

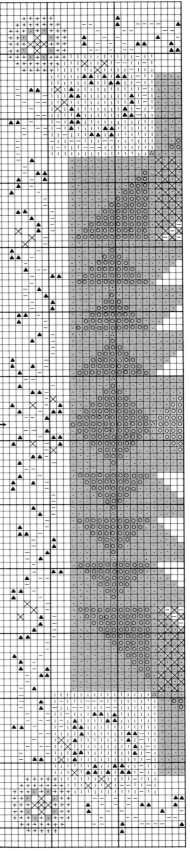

Stitch Count: 127 x 127

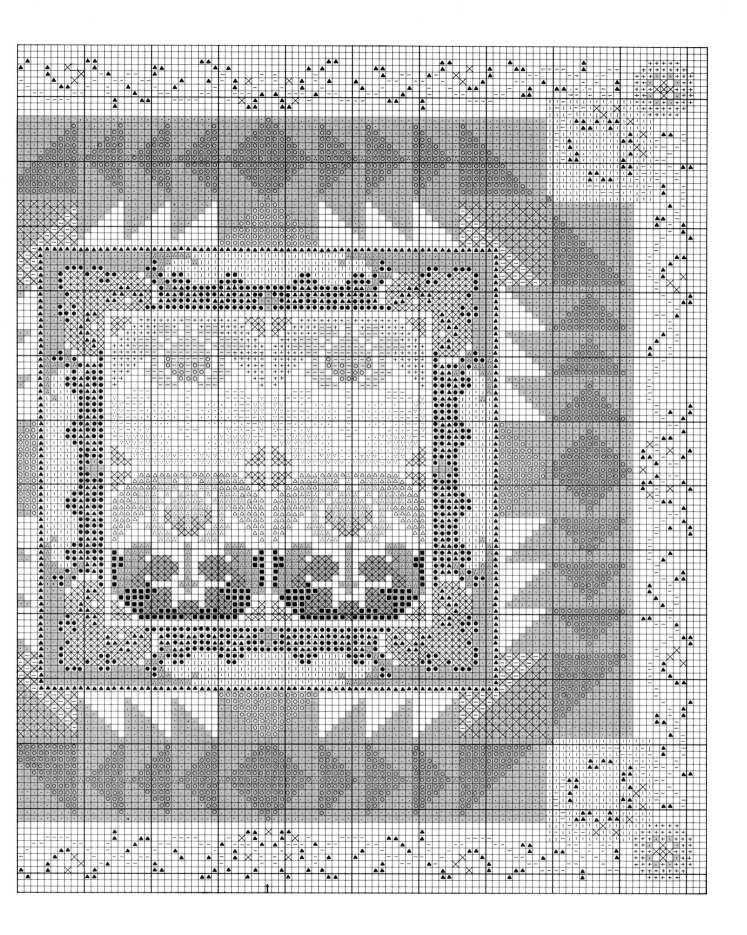

33

APRIL 11–12
Spring Farm Days

With those first warm spring days comes the promise of another growing season. During these days, at the Junior Museum in Tallahassee, Florida, the skills needed by colonial farm families are shown in needlework exhibits and wood-stove cooking, blacksmithing, and sheep-shearing demonstrations. Even if you don't live on a farm, you'll enjoy using this box topped with cross-stitched pictures of spring days.

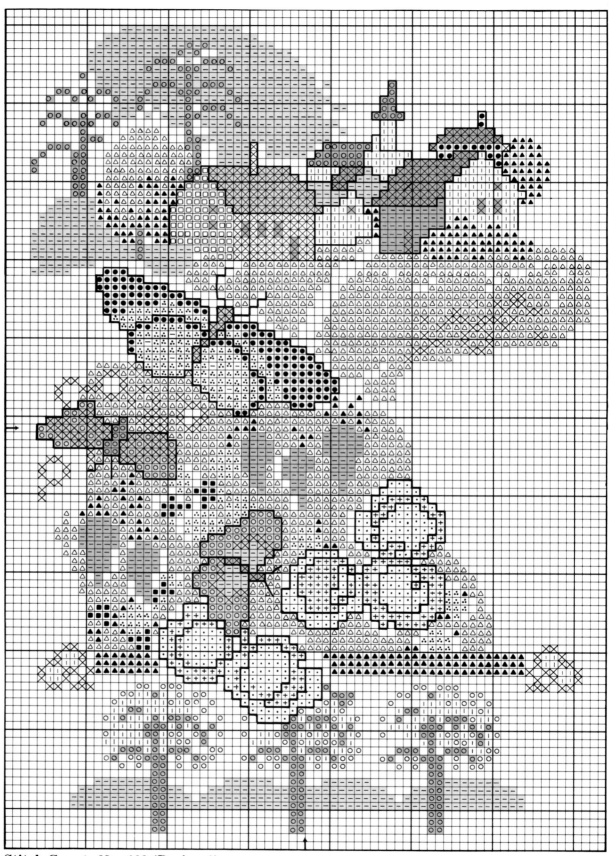

Stitch Count: 69 x 103 (Design 1)

Country Keepsake Box

SAMPLE for Design 1
Stitched on natural Super Linen 27 over 2 threads, the finished design size is 5¼" x 7⅝". The fabric was cut 12" x 14".

FABRICS	DESIGN SIZES
Aida 11	6⅜" x 9⅜"
Aida 14	5" x 7⅜"
Aida 18	3⅞" x 5¾"
Hardanger 22	3⅛" x 4⅝"

SAMPLE for Design 2
Stitched on natural Super Linen 27 over 2 threads, the finished design size is 5¼" x 7⅝". The fabric was cut 12" x 14".

FABRICS	DESIGN SIZES
Aida 11	6⅜" x 9⅜"
Aida 14	5" x 7⅜"
Aida 18	3⅞" x 5¾"
Hardanger 22	3⅛" x 4⅝"

MATERIALS
Completed cross-stitch on natural Super Linen 27
2 wooden frames (see step 1)
2 x 3-foot piece of ¼" plywood
Band saw
Sandpaper
Wood glue
½" finishing nails
Wood stain
Varnish
4 (¾") hinges
1 set of magnetic cabinet-closure hardware

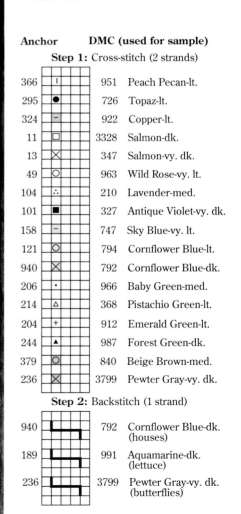

Anchor		DMC (used for sample)	
Step 1: Cross-stitch (2 strands)			
366	I	951	Peach Pecan-lt.
295	●	726	Topaz-lt.
324	−	922	Copper-lt.
11	□	3328	Salmon-dk.
13	⨯	347	Salmon-vy. dk.
49	O	963	Wild Rose-vy. lt.
104	∴	210	Lavender-med.
101	■	327	Antique Violet-vy. dk.
158	−	747	Sky Blue-vy. lt.
121	O	794	Cornflower Blue-lt.
940	⨯	792	Cornflower Blue-dk.
206	·	966	Baby Green-med.
214	△	368	Pistachio Green-lt.
204	+	912	Emerald Green-lt.
244	▲	987	Forest Green-dk.
379	O	840	Beige Brown-med.
236	⨯	3799	Pewter Gray-vy. dk.
Step 2: Backstitch (1 strand)			
940		792	Cornflower Blue-dk. (houses)
189		991	Aquamarine-dk. (lettuce)
236		3799	Pewter Gray-vy. dk. (butterflies)

DIRECTIONS

Note: Finished size of base: 15¼″ long by 10¾″ wide by 1⅞″ deep.

1. Have a professional framer construct frames for design pieces as follows: Molding is 1¼″-wide, ¾″-thick. Outside of each frame should measure 7⅝″ x 10¾″.

2. To make covers for backs of frames, measure opening of 1 frame back. Cut 2 pieces of plywood to these dimensions. Also from plywood, cut 2 (1⅞″ x 15¼″) pieces and 2 (1⅞″ x 10¼″) pieces for box sides, and 1 (10¾″ x 15¼″) piece for box bottom. Sand all pieces smooth.

3. Glue box sides together to form a 15¼″ x 10¾″ rectangle (see Diagram). Glue rectangle to box bottom. Let dry. Nail pieces together along edges to secure.

4. Stain and then varnish frames, frame backs, and box as desired.

5. Trim design pieces to 7½″ x 10½″ and mount in frames.

6. For framed cross-stitch doors, glue 1 frame back inside back opening of each framed piece. Referring to photo for position, hinge 1 frame to 1 side of box top, attaching 1 hinge 2″ from top corner and 1 hinge 2″ from bottom corner on outside of box. Repeat procedure for remaining frame. Attach the cabinet-closure hardware to the box and doors, following manufacturer's instructions.

Diagram

Anchor			DMC	(used for sample)
Step 1: Cross-stitch (2 strands)				
1	·	⁄		White
306	∣		725	Topaz
307	∴		977	Golden Brown-lt.
5975	□	◹	356	Terra Cotta-med.
871	+		3041	Antique Violet-med.
101	■		327	Antique Violet-vy. dk.
158	−	⁄	747	Sky Blue-vy. lt.
167	○		519	Sky Blue
779	✕		926	Slate Green
214	△		368	Pistachio Green-lt.
266	⁄		471	Avocado Green-vy. lt.
244	●	⁄•	987	Forest Green-dk.
379	−		840	Beige Brown-med.
905	○	⁄	645	Beaver Gray-vy. dk.
236	✕		3799	Pewter Gray-vy. dk.
Step 2: Backstitch (1 strand)				
236			3799	Pewter Gray-vy. dk.
Step 3: French Knot (1 strand)				
236	●		3799	Pewter Gray-vy. dk.

38

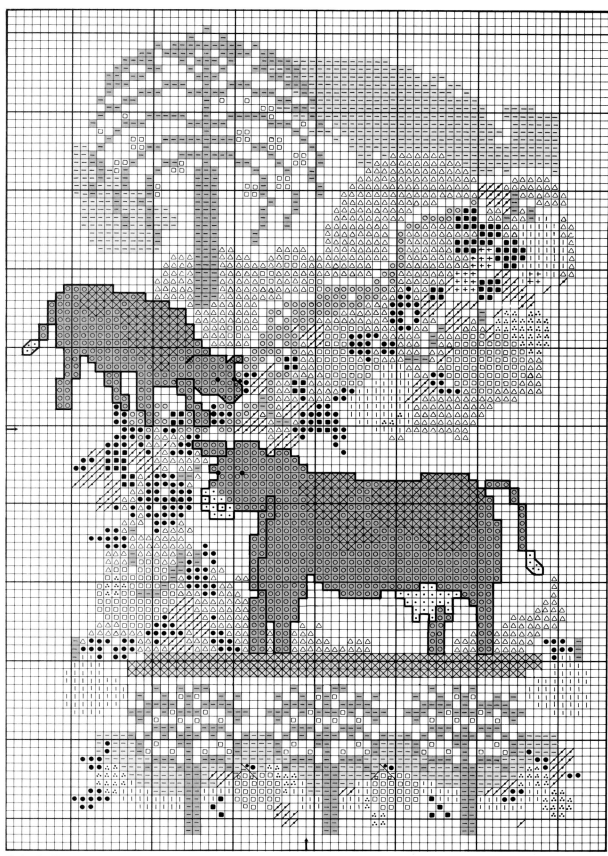

Stitch Count: 70 x 103 (Design 2)

APRIL 19

Easter

Simple woodworking and sponge painting blend with sweet cross-stitch to produce this floppy-eared bunny that is sure to hop into your heart on Easter morning.

Blossom Bunny

SAMPLE
Stitched on moss green Murano 30 over 2 threads, finished design size is 2⅛″ x 2½″ for 1 repeat. Fabric was cut 9″ x 25″. See Step 1 of Directions before stitching design.

FABRICS	DESIGN SIZES
Aida 11	2⅞″ x 3⅜″
Aida 14	2¼″ x 2⅝″
Aida 18	1¾″ x 2″
Hardanger 22	1⅜″ x 1⅝″

MATERIALS
- Completed cross-stitch on moss green Murano 30; matching thread
- 1 (9″ x 25″) piece of rose cotton fabric for ear lining
- 2 yards (⅛″-wide) light yellow satin ribbon
- 2 yards (1/16″-wide) pink satin ribbon
- 3 feet (8″-wide and ¾″-thick) pine
- Jigsaw
- Acrylic paints in pastel colors to coordinate with cross-stitch
- Natural sponges
- Baby's breath in assorted colors
- Wood glue, craft glue
- C-clamps
- Sandpaper
- Electric drill with ⅝″ bit
- Dressmakers' pen

DIRECTIONS
The pattern includes ¼″ seam allowance.

1. Transfer ear pattern to Murano. Begin stitching center of design at center of each ear, repeating motif to fill ear pattern. Cut out.

2. For ear lining, transfer ear pattern to rose fabric and cut out. To make ears, with right sides facing and raw edges aligned, stitch design piece to lining, leaving an opening for turning. Turn. Slipstitch opening closed.

3. To construct bunny, transfer patterns for body and legs to pine and cut out. Referring to pattern for placement, drill hole in bunny's head. Sand all wood pieces smooth. Using colors of choice, sponge-paint wood pieces by applying small amount of first paint to dry sponge and dabbing randomly on wood. Repeat with remaining colors, covering wood completely (see photo). Allow paint to dry.

Referring to Diagram, position legs on both sides of body and glue in place with wood glue. Then, secure legs to body with clamps to hold in position until glue is dry.

4. With craft glue, glue baby's breath around bunny's neck as desired (see photo). With design side up, insert and gently pull ear piece through hole in bunny's head so that ears are even.

5. To make bow, cut yellow and pink ribbons into 1-yard lengths. Handling all lengths as 1, tie ribbons in a bow around top of bunny's right ear close to head.

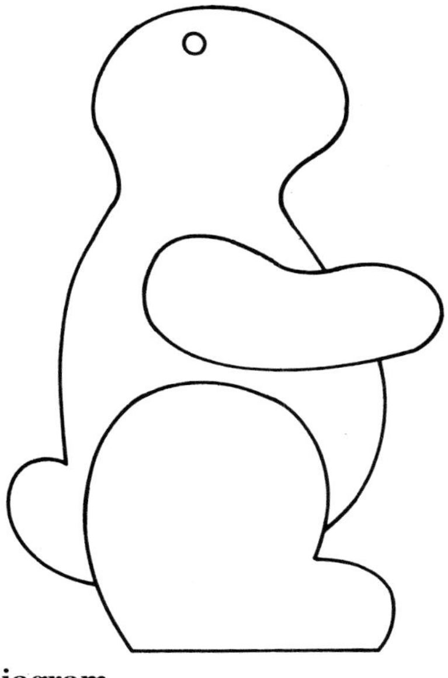

Diagram

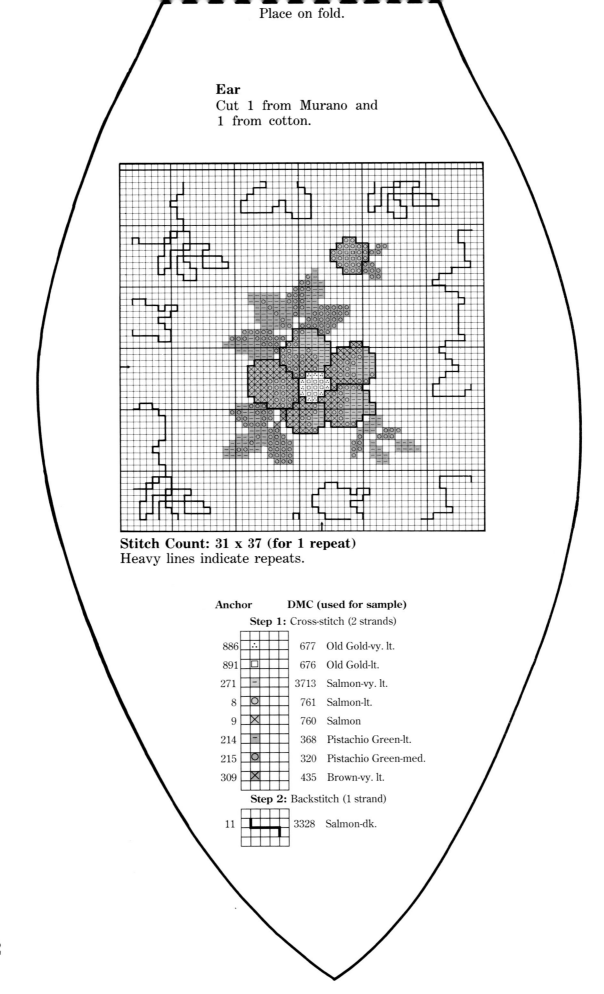

Place on fold.

Ear
Cut 1 from Murano and
1 from cotton.

Stitch Count: 31 x 37 (for 1 repeat)
Heavy lines indicate repeats.

Anchor   DMC (used for sample)

Step 1: Cross-stitch (2 strands)

Anchor		DMC	
886	∴	677	Old Gold-vy. lt.
891	□	676	Old Gold-lt.
271	–	3713	Salmon-vy. lt.
8	○	761	Salmon-lt.
9	✕	760	Salmon
214	–	368	Pistachio Green-lt.
215	○	320	Pistachio Green-med.
309	✕	435	Brown-vy. lt.

Step 2: Backstitch (1 strand)

11		3328	Salmon-dk.

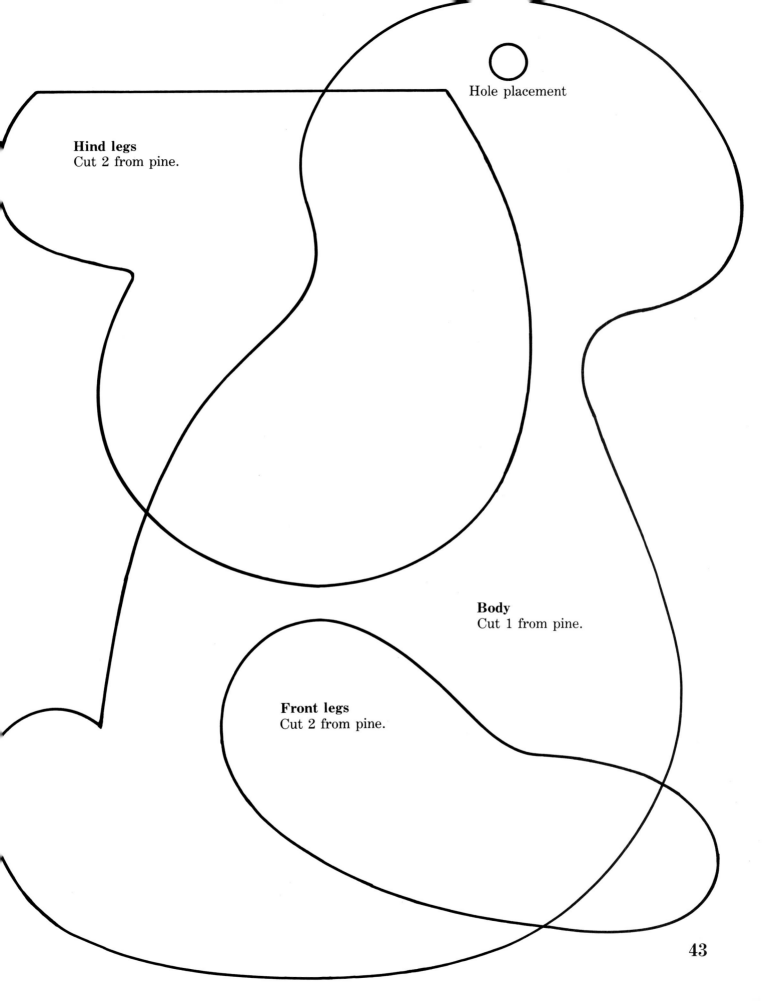

Hole placement

Hind legs
Cut 2 from pine.

Body
Cut 1 from pine.

Front legs
Cut 2 from pine.

43

MAY
Flower of the Month

Lilacs are among those twice-loved floral treasures—once for their beauty and once for their fragrance. A native of southeastern Europe, the lilac was one of the earliest transplants to be brought to North America.

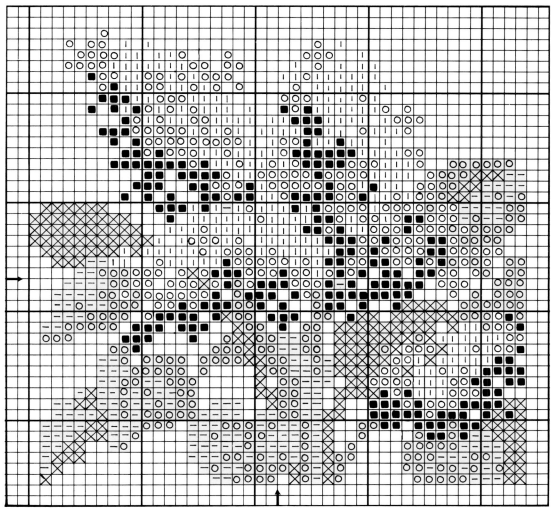

Stitch Count: 44 x 42

Afghan Square: Lilacs

SAMPLE

Stitched on Vanessa-Ann Afghan Weave 18 over 2 threads, the finished design size is 4⅞″ x 4⅝″. The fabric was cut 49″ x 59″ for complete afghan. See Suppliers for afghan material. Refer to page 10 for crochet instructions and for diagram showing placement of each design.

FABRICS	DESIGN SIZES
Aida 11	4″ x 3⅞″
Aida 14	3⅛″ x 3″
Aida 18	2½″ x 2⅜″
Hardanger 22	2″ x 1⅞″

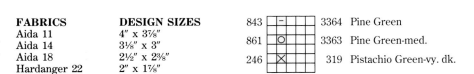

Anchor		DMC (used for sample)
	843	-	3364 Pine Green
	861	O	3363 Pine Green-med.
	246	X	319 Pistachio Green-vy. dk.

Step 1: Cross-stitch (3 strands)

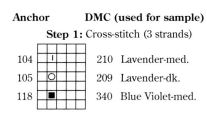

	Anchor		DMC (used for sample)
104		I	210 Lavender-med.
105		O	209 Lavender-dk.
118		■	340 Blue Violet-med.

MAY 10
Mother's Day

Stitched in soft pastels, this delicate design is as sweet and lovely as a mother's smile. The handmade ribbon flowers turn the simple needlepoint piece into a unique gift for Mom, making it the perfect token of your affection.

For Mom

SAMPLE

Stitched on Needlepoint Canvas 18 over 1 mesh, the finished design size is 3⅜″ x 3⅜″. The canvas was cut 11″ x 11″. See Suppliers for Overdyed floss.

MATERIALS

Completed stitching on Needlepoint Canvas 18
2⅞ yards (⅛″-wide) pink silk
  ribbon
1¾ yards (⅛″-wide) raspberry
  silk ribbon
1¾ yards (⅛″-wide) light blue
  silk ribbon
½ yard (⅛″-wide) pine green silk
  ribbon
½ yard (⅛″-wide) mint green silk
  ribbon
2 yards (¼″-wide) raspberry
  sparkle organdy ribbon
Thread to match ribbons
1 (8″) piece of pink floss
1 (1½″ x 2″) piece of heavy paper
  for tag
Craft glue
Tweezers

DIRECTIONS

1. After stitching is complete and before embellishing with leaves, ribbon roses, and bow, have a professional framer construct your mat and frame. The window should be cut in a 3¼″ x 5″ oval. Frame design piece, with side and bottom edges of design aligned with bottom half of window.

2. For ribbon roses, cut pink, raspberry, and light blue silk ribbon into 4″ pieces. For leaves, cut pine green and mint green silk ribbons into ¾″ pieces. For bow, cut 3 (24″) lengths of raspberry sparkle organdy ribbon.

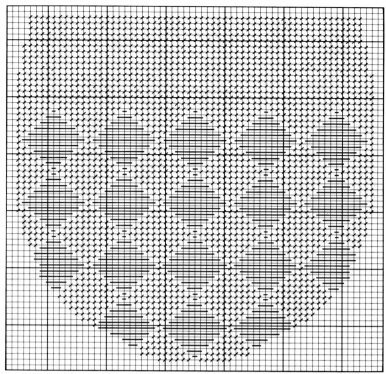

Stitch Count: 61 x 61

3. To make ribbon roses, tie a knot at 1 end of 1 piece of ribbon. Ravel opposite end slightly. With tweezers, pull 2 threads from center of opposite end of ribbon and gather ribbon tightly. Tack raw end to knot to secure rose. Repeat with remaining pieces. Set 2 roses aside to use in Step 7.

4. To make leaves, loop each piece of ribbon (see Diagram). Tack ends to secure. Set 4 leaves aside to use in Step 7.

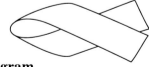

Diagram

5. Handling ribbon with tweezers and referring to photo, glue leaves randomly to unstitched canvas on top half of design piece. Allow to dry. Glue ribbon roses in place, covering ends of leaves and filling in unstitched canvas to complete oval shape (see photo).

6. To make bow, from lengths of organdy ribbon, tie 1 (1″-loop) bow, 1 (1½″-loop) bow, and 1 (2″-loop) bow, leaving long tails for streamers. Glue bows, 1 on top of the other from largest to smallest, ½″ below top center of oval.

7. Referring to photo, twist streamers and secure with glue as needed. Trim streamers at 3 different lengths. Glue reserved leaves and ribbon roses to center of layered bows.

8. Referring to photo, make gift tag and attach as desired.

Overdyed floss (used for sample)

Step 1: Continental Stitch (3 strands)

/		

182   Sandstone

Step 2: Satin Stitch (5 strands)

179   April Showers

MAY 17–23
World Trade Week

This well-traveled peddler celebrates the tradition of world trade in his trinket-adorned coat. In his hand is a special ornament gathered during one of his adventures.

Peddler Bear

SAMPLE for Ornament

Stitched on cream Hardanger 22 over 1 thread, the finished design size is 1⅞" x 1⅞". The fabric was cut 4" x 4".

To make ornament, glue scrap of fabric to wrong side of design piece. Varnish both sides. Pin edges to waxed paper; let dry. Trim design ⅛" outside stitching. Varnish again, covering raw edges thoroughly. Spray with glitter spray.

FABRICS	DESIGN SIZES
Aida 11	3⅞" x 3⅞"
Aida 14	3" x 3"
Aida 18	2⅜" x 2⅜"

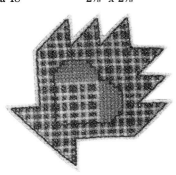

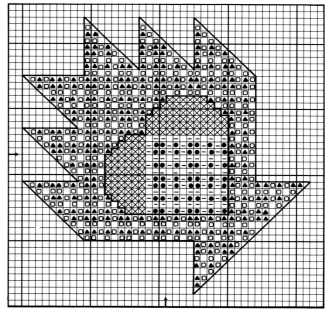

Stitch Count: 42 x 42

Anchor	DMC (used for sample)		
Step 1: Cross-stitch (1 strand)			
893	−	224	Shell Pink-lt.
894	✕	223	Shell Pink-med.
897	●	221	Shell Pink-vy. dk.
920	□	932	Antique Blue-lt.
922	▲	930	Antique Blue-dk.

Step 2: Backstitch (1 strand)

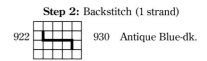

922 · · · · · 930 Antique Blue-dk.

49

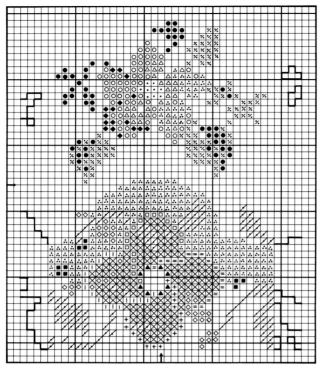

Stitch Count: 33 x 50
(for 1 repeat)

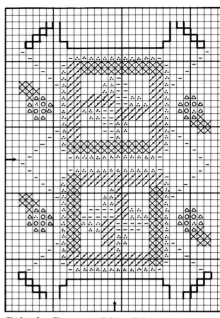

Stitch Count: 28 x 34
(for 1 repeat)

SAMPLE for Coat
Stitched on cracked wheat Murano 30 over 2 threads, the finished design size is 2¼″ x 3⅜″ for 1 repeat. The fabric was cut 27″ x 12¼″ for complete design. Begin stitching so that left bottom corner of design is 3⅜″ from left edge of fabric and 3¾″ from bottom of fabric. Repeat design 10 times horizontally as indicated by heavy lines on graph.

FABRICS	DESIGN SIZES
Aida 11	3″ x 4½″
Aida 14	2⅜″ x 3⅝″
Aida 18	1⅞″ x 2¾″
Hardanger 22	1½″ x 2¼″

Anchor		DMC (used for sample)	
		Step 1: Cross-stitch (2 strands)	
890	·	729	Old Gold-med.
42	△	3350	Dusty Rose-dk.
896	∴	3722	Shell Pink
896	○	3721	Shell Pink-dk.
70	■	3685	Mauve-dk.
72	◆	902	Garnet-vy. dk.
870	□	3042	Antique Violet-lt.
154	=	3755	Baby Blue
167	I	3766	Peacock Blue-lt.
236	▲	3799	Pewter Gray-vy. dk.
185	+	964	Seagreen-lt.
189	●	991	Aquamarine-dk.
266	╱	3347	Yellow Green-med.
243	╱.	988	Forest Green-med.
862	◇	3362	Pine Green-dk.
899	✕	3782	Mocha Brown-lt.

SAMPLE for Placket Band
Stitched on moss green Murano 30 over 2 threads, the finished design size is 1⅞″ x 2¼″ for 1 repeat. The fabric was cut 7¾″ x 12¼″ for complete design. Begin stitching so that right bottom corner of design is 3⅜″ from right edge of fabric and 3⅝″ from bottom edge of fabric. Repeat design 3 times vertically as indicated by heavy lines on graph, leaving 2⅛″ of fabric unstitched at top.

FABRICS	DESIGN SIZES
Aida 11	2½″ x 3⅛″
Aida 14	2″ x 2⅜″
Aida 18	1½″ x 1⅞″
Hardanger 22	1¼″ x 1½″

Anchor		DMC (used for sample)	
		Step 1: Cross-stitch (2 strands)	
271	△	3713	Salmon-vy. lt.
75	○	3733	Dusty Rose-lt.
76	∴	3731	Dusty Rose-med.
871	╱	3041	Antique Violet-med.
875	–	503	Blue Green-med.
859	✕	3052	Green Gray-med.

MATERIALS

Completed cross-stitch on moss green Murano 30 (placket band)
Completed cross-stitch on cracked wheat Murano 30 (coat)
Completed ornament (see Sample information)
Scrap of tan print fabric (1 sleeve)
Scrap of brown print fabric (1 sleeve)
¼ yard of rose fabric (binding)
Knit baby cap in desired color
1 (17″-high) stuffed bear with 14″ waist
Metal display stand
½ yard (¼″-wide) elastic
Cream thread
2 (⅝″-wide) wooden beads
Assorted buttons, beads, trinkets, and ornaments (see photo)

DIRECTIONS

The patterns include ¼″ seam allowances.

1. For coat, trim 3″ from left and 3″ from bottom edges only. For placket band, trim 3″ from right and 3″ from bottom edges only.

2. To make coat, enlarge pattern and cut out. With side and bottom edges aligned, place pattern on finished design piece and cut out.

3. To attach placket band, place design edge of band on left coat front, with right sides facing and raw edges aligned. Stitch together along long edge. Open out fabric. To hem bottom edge, turn under ¼″ twice on placket band and coat and stitch. On remaining long edge of placket band, turn under seam allowance and press. With wrong sides facing, fold placket in half to form self facing. Slipstitch facing to inside of coat over seam line.

On the right edge of the coat, fold ¼″ and then 1½″ to the wrong side to make self facing and press.

Slipstitch the facing in place.

Make ¼″ tucks around neck edge of coat, placing 4 in back and 2 on each side of coat front.

4. To make sleeves, cut 1 (8½″ x 6½″) piece from each print fabric. With right sides facing and raw edges aligned, fold 1 piece in half widthwise and stitch long edges together. Turn. Sew a ¼″ hem on 1 end. With right sides facing and raw edges aligned, stitch sleeve to coat, easing fabric as needed. Repeat for other sleeve.

5. To bind neck of coat, cut 1″-wide bias strips from rose fabric, piecing as needed to equal 19″. Leaving a 4″ tail at each end, bind neck of coat. Thread 1 wooden bead on each tail and knot ends to secure (see photo).

6. To make pants, transfer pattern to rose fabric and cut out. With right sides facing and raw edges aligned, stitch inseam on each piece. With right sides facing and raw edges aligned, stitch pieces together along center front and back seam. To make casing for cuffs, fold bottom edge of each leg ½″ to wrong side. Topstitch close to raw edge, leaving an opening. Make a casing for waist in same manner. Thread 1 (3″) piece of elastic through each casing in legs; overlap ends ½″ and stitch. Slipstitch opening closed. Repeat for waist, using 9½″ piece of elastic.

7. Attach a button to hat cuff (see photo). Dress bear in pants, coat, and cap. Attach bear to metal stand. Embellish coat as desired. Pin ornament to bear's hand.

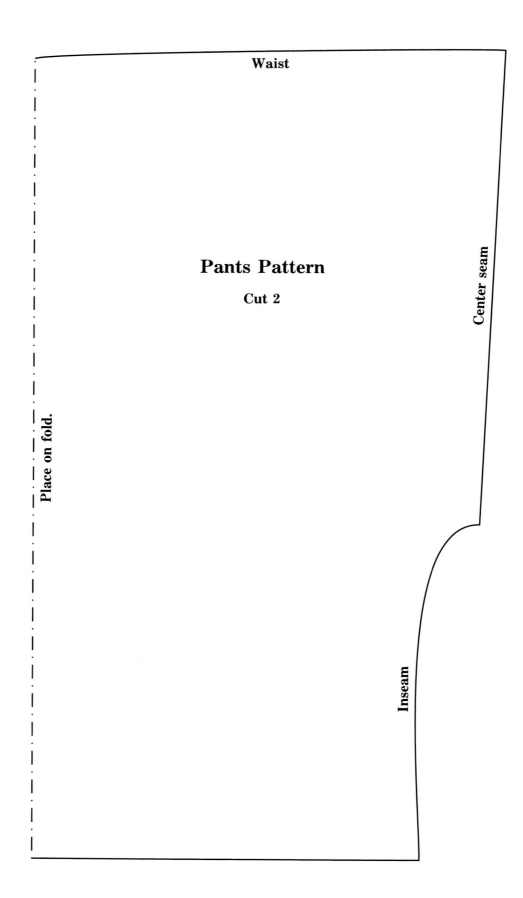

Waist

Center seam

Pants Pattern

Cut 2

Place on fold.

Inseam

52

Place on fold.

Coat Pattern

Each square = 1″.

JUNE
Flower of the Month

Tulips are graceful garden flowers that grow in many parts of the world, especially the Netherlands. Their simplicity lends itself both to children's drawings and to elegant arrangements.

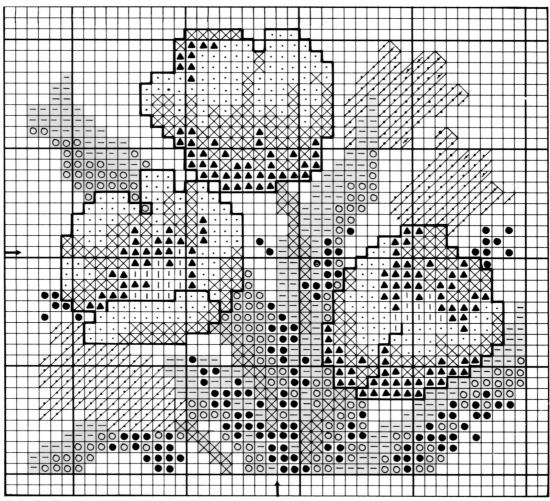

Stitch Count: 44 x 41

Afghan Square: Tulips

SAMPLE

Stitched on Vanessa-Ann Afghan Weave 18 over 2 threads, the finished design size is 4⅞" x 4½". The fabric was cut 49" x 59" for complete afghan. See Suppliers for afghan material. Refer to page 10 for crochet instructions and for diagram showing placement of each design.

FABRICS	DESIGN SIZES
Aida 11	4" x 3¾"
Aida 14	3⅛" x 2⅞"
Aida 18	2½" x 2¼"
Hardanger 22	2" x 1⅞"

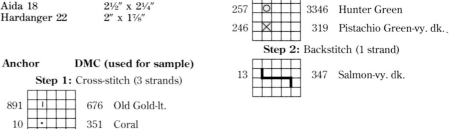

Anchor		DMC (used for sample)	
Step 1: Cross-stitch (3 strands)			
891	I	676	Old Gold-lt.
10	·	351	Coral
11	X	350	Coral-med.
13	▲	347	Salmon-vy. dk.
76	╱	3731	Dusty Rose-med.
118	●	340	Blue Violet-med.
242	–	989	Forest Green
257	O	3346	Hunter Green
246	X	319	Pistachio Green-vy. dk.
Step 2: Backstitch (1 strand)			
13	⌐	347	Salmon-vy. dk.

JUNE 12–14
Sea Music Festival

The seaport of Mystic, Connecticut, begins each June with a grand celebration. Music soars from the ships in the harbor, while visitors enjoy various workshops and concerts. This colorful piece depicts the creatures beneath the sea having a festival of their own.

Stitch Count: 269 x 126

Fish Festival

SAMPLE
Stitched on cream Belfast Linen 32 over 2 threads, the finished design size is 16¾" x 7⅞". The fabric was cut 23" x 14".

FABRICS	DESIGN SIZES
Aida 11	24½" x 11½"
Aida 14	19¼" x 9"
Aida 18	15" x 7"
Hardanger 22	12¼" x 5¾"

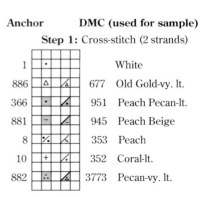

Anchor			DMC (used for sample)
Step 1: Cross-stitch (2 strands)			
1	·		White
886	△	◿	677 Old Gold-vy. lt.
366	·	◿	951 Peach Pecan-lt.
881	−	◿	945 Peach Beige
8	⁒	◿	353 Peach
10	+	◿	352 Coral-lt.
882	∴	◿	3773 Pecan-vy. lt.

337			3778	Terra Cotta
27			893	Carnation-lt.
969			3727	Antique Mauve-lt.
870			3042	Antique Violet-lt.
871			3041	Antique Violet-med.
117			3747	Blue Violet-vy. lt.
118			341	Blue Violet-lt.
928			598	Turquoise-lt.
167			597	Turquoise

168			518	Wedgewood-lt.
978			322	Navy Blue-vy. lt.
816			3750	Antique Blue-vy. dk.
213			369	Pistachio Green-vy. lt.
214			368	Pistachio Green-lt.
875			503	Blue Green-med.
397			762	Pearl Gray-vy. lt.

Step 2: Backstitch (1 strand)

1			White (peach fish's eye)
882		3773	Pecan-vy. lt. (starfish and shells)
816		3750	Antique Blue-vy. dk. (all else)

Step 3: French Knot (1 strand)

| 1 | | | White |
| 816 | | 3750 | Antique Blue-vy. dk. |

JUNE 21
Summer Solstice

This day marks the beginning of summer in the northern hemisphere. We honor it with a cross-stitched sun face glittering with gold metallic thread.

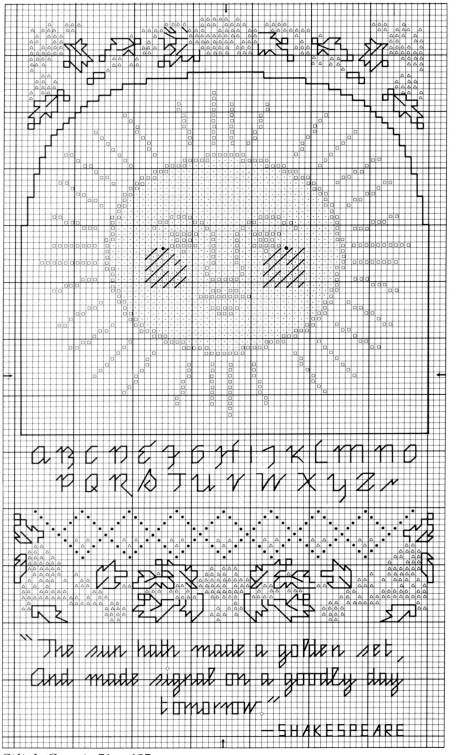

Stitch Count: 71 x 127

A Golden Set

SAMPLE

Stitched on yellow Petit Point Canvas 22 over 2 threads, the finished design size is 6½" x 11½". The canvas was cut 13" x 18". See Suppliers for gold Madeira.

FABRICS	DESIGN SIZES
Aida 11	6½" x 11½"
Aida 14	5⅛" x 9⅛"
Aida 18	4" x 7"
Hardanger 22	3¼" x 5¾"

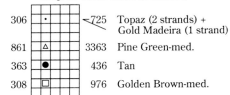

Anchor		DMC (used for sample)

Step 1: Cross-stitch (2 strands)

306	·	725	Topaz (2 strands) + Gold Madeira (1 strand)
861	△	3363	Pine Green-med.
363	●	436	Tan
308	□	976	Golden Brown-med.

Step 2: Backstitch (1 strand)

861		3363	Pine Green-med. (leaves)
370		434	Brown-lt. (inside sun, border around sun)
371		433	Brown-med. (alphabet)
357		801	Coffee Brown-dk. (all else)

Step 3: French Knot (1 strand)

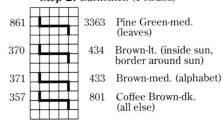

308	●	976	Golden Brown-med.
357	⊕	801	Coffee Brown-dk.

J U L Y
Flower of the Month

During summer's hottest days, Mother Nature brightens some un-likely corners of the world with wild roses. These hardy beauties are found in open prairies and pastures, in dry woods and fields, and on rocky hillsides.

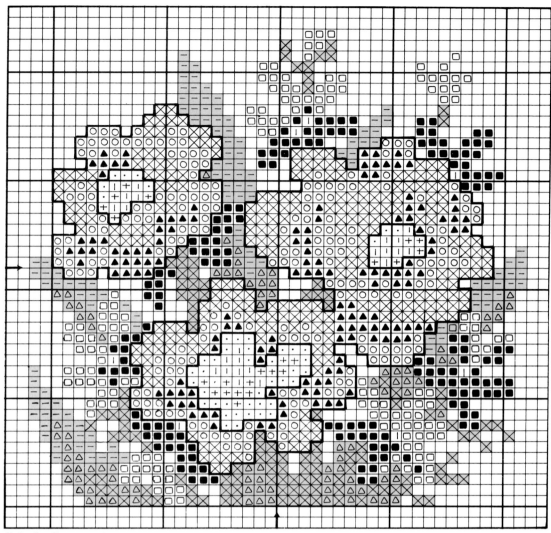

Stitch Count: 44 x 44

Afghan Square: Wild Roses

SAMPLE

Stitched on Vanessa-Ann Afghan Weave 18 over 2 threads, the finished design size is 4⅞″ x 4⅞″. The fabric was cut 49″ x 59″ for complete afghan. See Suppliers for afghan material. Refer to page 10 for crochet instructions and for diagram showing placement of each design.

FABRICS	DESIGN SIZES
Aida 11	4″ x 4″
Aida 14	3⅛″ x 3⅛″
Aida 18	2½″ x 2½″
Hardanger 22	2″ x 2″

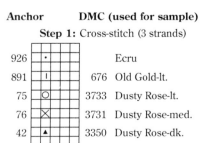

Anchor		DMC (used for sample)

Step 1: Cross-stitch (3 strands)

926	·	Ecru
891	I	676 Old Gold-lt.
75	O	3733 Dusty Rose-lt.
76	X	3731 Dusty Rose-med.
42	▲	3350 Dusty Rose-dk.

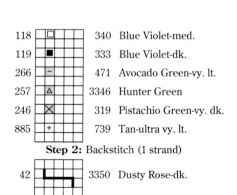

118	□	340 Blue Violet-med.
119	■	333 Blue Violet-dk.
266	–	471 Avocado Green-vy. lt.
257	△	3346 Hunter Green
246	X	319 Pistachio Green-vy. dk.
885	+	739 Tan-ultra vy. lt.

Step 2: Backstitch (1 strand)

42		3350 Dusty Rose-dk.

Independence Day

Add a touch of American pride to your home with these patriotic ornaments. They will be a reminder to everybody of our nation's great achievements.

American Pride

SAMPLE for Lady Liberty
Stitched on cream Plastic Canvas 14 over 1 mesh, the finished design size is ⅝" x 1¾" for 1 arm, 2¾" x ¾" for skirt ruffle, and 3⅜" x 4" for body. Use 1 (4" x 4") sheet of plastic canvas for arms and ruffle and 1 (4" x 4") sheet for body. Begin stitching body design on far left edge of canvas, working across to the right. When stitching is complete, there should be about ⅜" unstitched canvas remaining. Bold lines on graphs for arms, skirt ruffle, and skirt edges indicate cutting lines. See General Instructions for information on working with plastic canvas. See Suppliers for plastic canvas.

MATERIALS for Lady Liberty
Completed cross-stitch on Plastic Canvas 14
9" of matching light blue yarn
5 oval gold beads
1 red plastic star bead

DIRECTIONS
1. On plastic canvas of each arm piece, skirt ruffle, and skirt edge, mark very lightly with pencil where bold lines occur on graph. Carefully cut canvas along pencil lines, rounding out curves where necessary.

2. Cut armholes in plastic canvas where blank rows appear on graph. (Bold lines indicate cutting lines.) Overcast edges of all pieces including armholes (see step 5 of color code). Insert, at an angle, 1 arm into each armhole (see photo). Whipstitch each arm to body at point of insertion.

3. Whipstitch beads to bottom of skirt at ½" intervals (see photo). Stitch star to top center of crown. Center skirt ruffle under bottom of skirt and whipstitch in place on back.

4. Roll design into a cylinder, creating an overlap in back with unstitched portion of plastic canvas underneath; whipstitch. To make hanger, stitch matching floss across diameter of top of cylinder to form an asterisk. Tie 9" piece of yarn around center of asterisk where floss crosses, pull ends even, and knot.

Anchor   DMC (used for sample)

Step 1: Cross-stitch (3 strands)

926		Ecru
306		725 Topaz
896	○	3722 Shell Pink
59	✕	326 Rose-vy. dk.
343		3752 Antique Blue-ultra vy. lt.
149		311 Navy Blue-med.
885	−	739 Tan-ultra vy. lt.
830		644 Beige Gray-med.
382	●	3021 Brown Gray-vy. dk.

Step 2: Backstitch (1 strand)

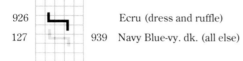

926		Ecru (dress and ruffle)
127		939 Navy Blue-vy. dk. (all else)

Step 3: French Knot (1 strand)

127	▲	939 Navy Blue-vy. dk.

Step 4: Beadwork

	△	Red star
		Long oval beads

Step 5: Cut and Overcast (3 strands)
(see Steps 1 and 2 of Directions)

926		Ecru (dress ruffle)
59		326 Rose-vy. dk. (bottom of dress)
343		3752 Antique Blue-ultra vy. lt. (background)
149		311 Navy Blue-med. (sleeves)
885		739 Tan-ultra vy. lt. (hands)

Stitch Count: 48 x 57 (for body)

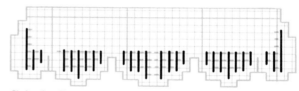

Stitch Count: 38 x 11 (for skirt ruffle)

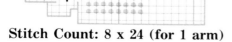

Stitch Count: 8 x 24 (for 1 arm)

Stitch Count: 50 x 57 (for body)

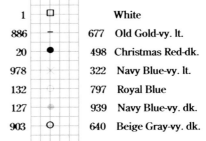
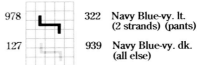

SAMPLE for Uncle Sam

Stitched on cream Plastic Canvas 14 over 1 mesh, the finished design size is ⅝" x 1¾" for 1 arm, ⅝" x ¾" for 1 leg, and 3⅝" x 4" for body. Use 1 (4" x 4") sheet of plastic canvas for arms and legs and 1 (4" x 4") sheet for body. Begin stitching body design on far left edge of canvas, working across to the right. When stitching is complete, there should be about ⅜" unstitched canvas remaining. Bold lines on graphs for arms and legs indicate cutting lines. See General Instructions for information on working with plastic canvas. See Suppliers for plastic canvas.

MATERIALS for Uncle Sam

Completed cross-stitch on Plastic
  Canvas 14
Toothpick flag
9" of matching dark brown yarn

DIRECTIONS

1. On plastic canvas of each arm and leg piece, mark very lightly with a pencil where bold lines occur on graph. Carefully cut canvas along pencil lines, rounding out curves where necessary.

2. Cut armholes in plastic canvas where blank rows appear on graph. (Bold lines indicate cutting lines.) Overcast edges of all pieces, including armholes (see step 4 of color code).

3. Whipstitch flag onto 1 hand. Attach arms as for Lady Liberty (see photo). Whipstitch legs to back of design with legs protruding ⁹⁄₁₆". To finish ornament, see Lady Liberty, step 4.

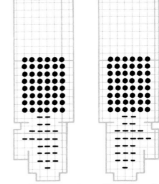

Stitch Count: 8 x 25 (for 1 arm)

Stitch Count: 8 x 10 (for 1 leg)

SAMPLE for Log Cabin

Stitched on cream Plastic Canvas 14 over 1 mesh, the finished design size is 3⅛" x 1¼" for 1 roof panel, 3⅛" x 1⅝" for bottom, 1⅝" x 2⅞" for 1 side panel, 3⅛" x 2¼" for back, and 3⅛" x 2¼" for front. Use 5 (4" x 4") pieces of plastic canvas to complete log cabin. Stitch 2 side panels and 2 roof panels. Bold lines on graphs indicate cutting lines. See General Instructions for information on working with plastic canvas. See Suppliers for plastic canvas.

MATERIALS for Log Cabin

Completed cross-stitch on Plastic Canvas 14
Scrap of foam-core board
Scrap of brown paper
White glue
Hot-glue gun and glue sticks
Craft knife

DIRECTIONS

1. On plastic canvas, for each design piece, mark very lightly with pencil where bold lines occur on graph. Carefully cut along pencil lines.

2. Overcast edges of all cabin pieces (see step 3 of color code). Whipstitch front and back to sides, roof panels together along long top edges, and then roof to top edges of cabin. Turn cabin upside down and whipstitch bottom to cabin.

3. To make chimney, transfer pattern onto foam-core board and cut out with craft knife. Wrap chimney with brown paper, trimming as needed to fit. Overlap paper at back and glue. Using glue gun, glue chimney to right side of house (see photo).

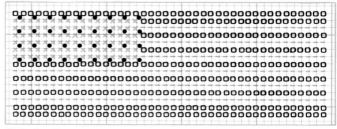

Stitch Count: 44 x 17
(for 1 roof panel)

44 x 31 (for front)

44 x 31 (for back)

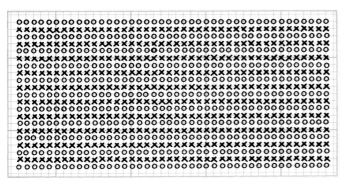

44 x 23 (for bottom)

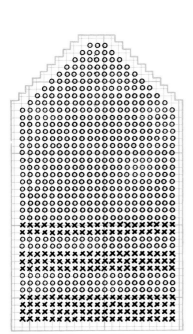

23 x 41 (for 1 side)

Chimney Pattern

Anchor		DMC (used for sample)

Step 1: Cross-stitch (3 strands)

1			White
59	□	326	Rose-vy. dk.
872	−	3740	Antique Violet-dk.
343	⊕	3752	Antique Blue-ultra vy. lt.
149	╳	311	Navy Blue-med.
840	⊟	3768	Slate Green-dk.
373	O	422	Hazel Nut Brown-lt.
375	✕	420	Hazel Nut Brown-dk.
382	▪	3021	Brown Gray-vy. dk.

Step 2: French Knot (2 strands)

1	●	White

Step 3: Cut and overcast (3 strands)
(see Steps 1 and 2 of Directions)

59		326	Rose-vy. dk.
373		422	Hazel Nut Brown-lt.
375		420	Hazel Nut Brown-dk.

AUGUST
Flower of the Month

**Poppies are sometimes called the show-off flower. After all, they can
hardly be overlooked, with their brilliant colors, bold accent in the
center, and large size. They may grow as big as a foot across.**

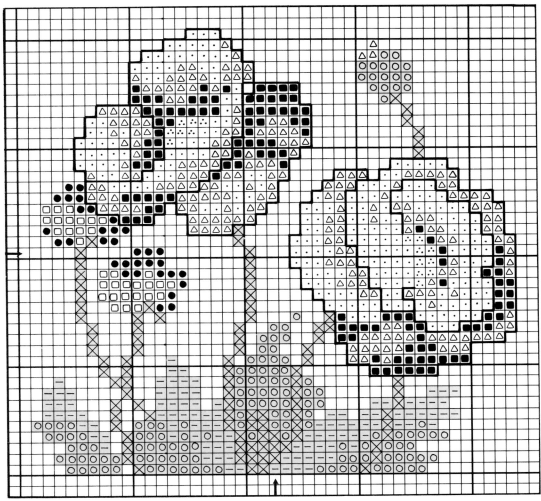

Stitch Count: 43 x 41

Afghan Square: Poppies

SAMPLE
Stitched on Vanessa-Ann Afghan Weave 18 over 2 threads, the finished design size is 4⅞″ x 4½″. The fabric was cut 49″ x 59″ for complete afghan. See Suppliers for afghan material. Refer to page 10 for crochet instructions and for diagram showing placement of each design.

FABRICS
Aida 11
Aida 14
Aida 18
Hardanger 22

DESIGN SIZES
4″ x 3¾″
3⅛″ x 2⅞″
2⅜″ x 2¼″
2″ x 1⅞″

Anchor		DMC (used for sample)	
	Step 1:	Cross-stitch (3 strands)	
10	·	352	Coral-lt.
11	△	350	Coral-med.
13	■	347	Salmon-vy. dk.
75	□	3733	Dusty Rose-lt.
76	●	3731	Dusty Rose-med.

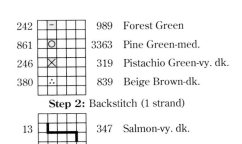

242	−	989	Forest Green
861	○	3363	Pine Green-med.
246	✕	319	Pistachio Green-vy. dk.
380	∴	839	Beige Brown-dk.

Step 2: Backstitch (1 strand)

13		347	Salmon-vy. dk.

AUGUST 7
Six Nations Indian Pageant

Each year, Native Americans on the Six Nations Reserve in Oshweken, Ontario, gather to honor their culture and history. Our cross-stitch banner, depicting an Indian mother and child, pays tribute to those traditions.

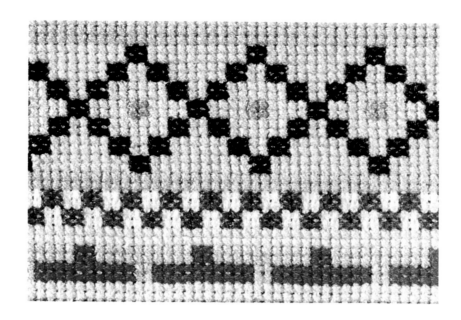

Indian Mother and Child

SAMPLE

Stitched on natural Aida 14 over 1 thread, the finished design size is 11⅜″ x 22″. The fabric was cut 18″ x 31″. Begin stitching at the top center of the design, 3″ from top edge of fabric.

FABRICS	DESIGN SIZES
Aida 11	14½″ x 28″
Aida 18	8⅞″ x 17″
Hardanger 22	7¼″ x 14″

MATERIALS

Completed cross-stitch on natural Aida 14; matching thread
1 (17⅜″ x 31″) piece of unstitched natural Aida 14 for back
Batting
1 (24″-long) arrow
2½ yards (⅛″-wide) tan leather bootlace
Lambswool for trim
Feathers
Wooden and ceramic beads in colors to complement design

DIRECTIONS

All seam allowances are ¼″.

1. Trim design piece as follows: Leave a 3″ margin at top and a 1″ margin on each side. Using bottom of design as a guide and leaving a 5½″ margin, trim bottom edge (see photo). From batting, cut 1 (13⅜″ x 26″) piece.

2. With top and side edges aligned, pin batting to wrong side of design piece. Baste in place. With right sides facing and raw edges aligned, stitch design piece to back, leaving bottom edge open. Clip corners and trim batting seam allowances. Turn.

3. Topstitch through all 3 layers along bottom edge of design. (Front and back will extend below topstitching and will be used for fringe.) Trim batting close to stitching.

4. To make fringe, ravel Aida by removing horizontal threads on front and back up to topstitching. Beginning at left edge, group threads, ½″ section at a time, and knot close to topstitching. Work across to right edge (see photo).

5. Fold top edge of design piece over arrow and slipstitch to back.

6. To make hanger, cut 1 yard of bootlace. Tie 1 end of bootlace to 1 end of arrow. Repeat on opposite end.

7. Embellish as desired, using remaining leather bootlace, lambswool, feathers, and wooden and ceramic beads (see photo).

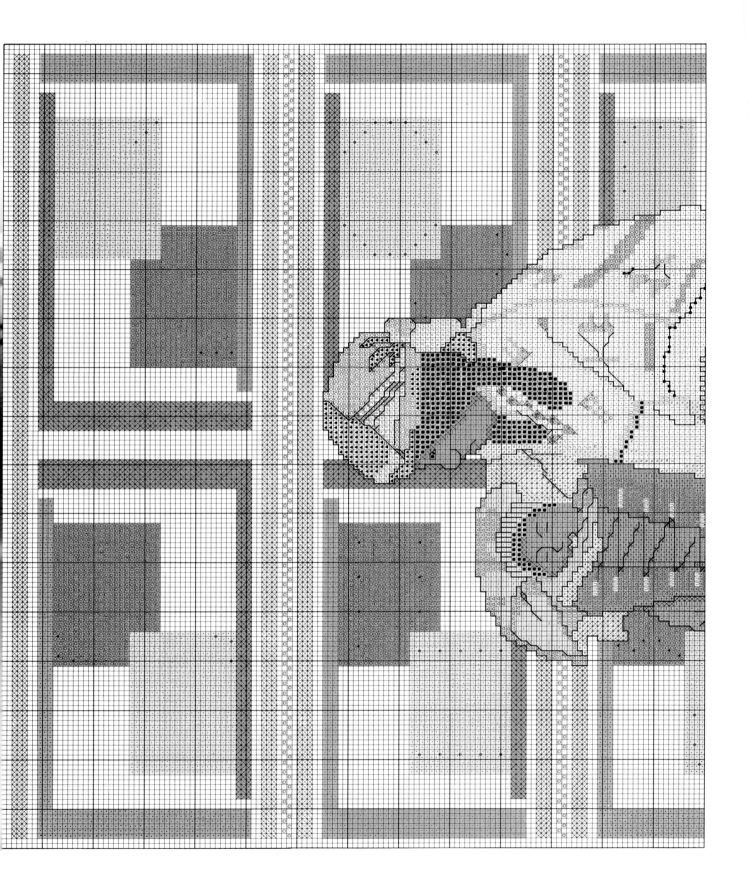

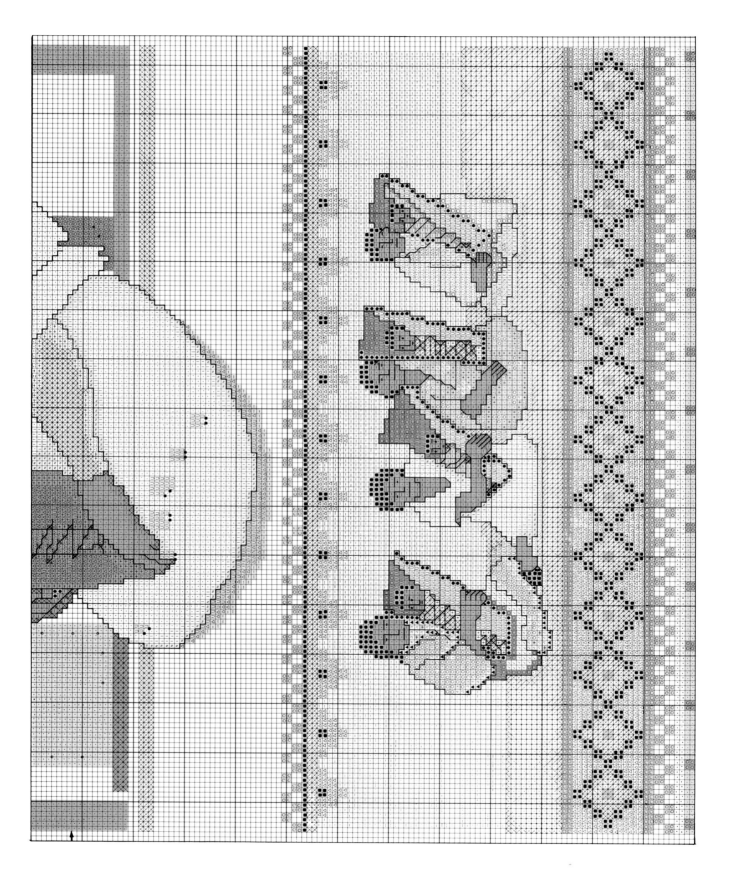

Stitch Count: 160 x 308

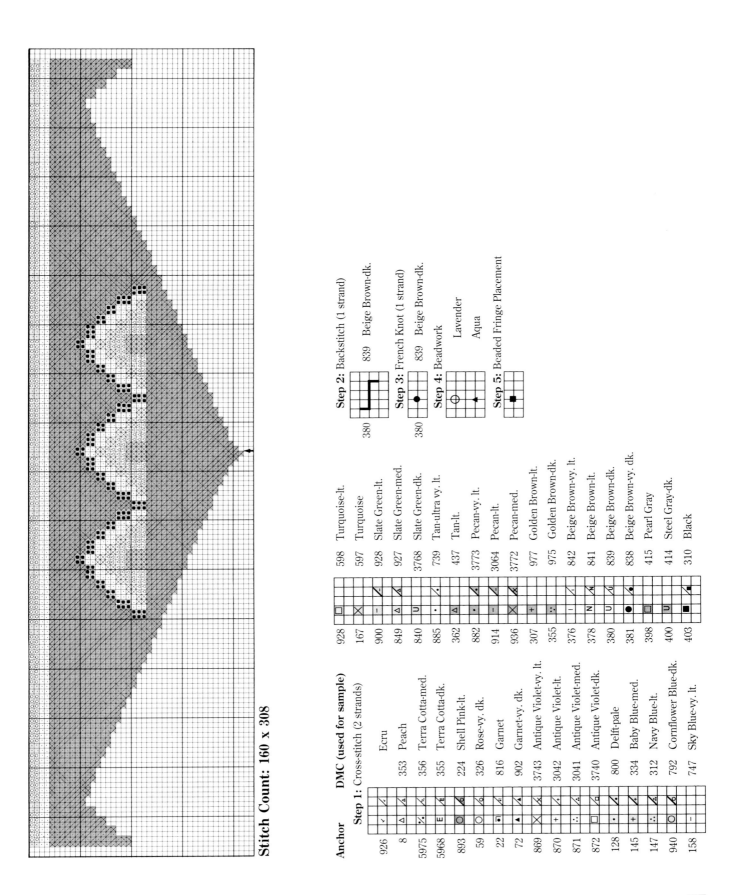

Anchor	DMC (used for sample)
Step 1: Cross-stitch (2 strands)	
926	Ecru
8	353 Peach
5975	356 Terra Cotta-med.
5968	355 Terra Cotta-dk.
893	224 Shell Pink-lt.
59	326 Rose-vy. dk.
22	816 Garnet
72	902 Garnet-vy. dk.
869	3743 Antique Violet-vy. lt.
870	3042 Antique Violet-lt.
871	3041 Antique Violet-med.
872	3740 Antique Violet-dk.
128	800 Delft-pale
145	334 Baby Blue-med.
147	312 Navy Blue-lt.
940	792 Cornflower Blue-dk.
158	747 Sky Blue-vy. lt.

Anchor	DMC (used for sample)
928	598 Turquoise-lt.
167	597 Turquoise
900	928 Slate Green-lt.
849	927 Slate Green-med.
840	3768 Slate Green-dk.
885	739 Tan-ultra vy. lt.
362	437 Tan-lt.
882	3773 Pecan-vy. lt.
914	3064 Pecan-lt.
936	3772 Pecan-med.
307	977 Golden Brown-lt.
355	975 Golden Brown-dk.
376	842 Beige Brown-vy. lt.
378	841 Beige Brown-lt.
380	839 Beige Brown-dk.
381	838 Beige Brown-vy. dk.
398	415 Pearl Gray
400	414 Steel Gray-dk.
403	310 Black

Step 2: Backstitch (1 strand)
380 839 Beige Brown-dk.

Step 3: French Knot (1 strand)
380 839 Beige Brown-dk.

Step 4: Beadwork
⊕ Lavender
◆ Aqua

Step 5: Beaded Fringe Placement
■

Baby Parade

"Hush! Baby's bearly sheepin," says one of these cute bibs, on which a bear cub rides a rocking lamb. Probably not many babies will be "sheepin" at the baby parade in Ocean City, New Jersey, the oldest on the East Coast. More likely, they'll be wanting to eat—and with these clever button-on bibs, they'll be ready.

Bears on Parade

SAMPLE for Design 1
Stitched on apricot Pastel Linen 28 over 2 threads, the finished design size is 3¾" x 7⅛". The fabric was cut 10" x 13".

FABRICS	DESIGN SIZES
Aida 11	4¾" x 9"
Aida 14	3¾" x 7⅛"
Aida 18	2⅞" x 5½"
Hardanger 22	2⅜" x 4½"

SAMPLE for Design 2
Stitched on periwinkle Pastel Linen 28 over 2 threads, the finished design size is 4" x 7". The fabric was cut 10" x 13".

FABRICS	DESIGN SIZES
Aida 11	5⅛" x 8⅞"
Aida 14	4" x 7"
Aida 18	3⅛" x 5⅛"
Hardanger 22	2½" x 4½"

MATERIALS (for 1 bib)
Completed cross-stitch on Pastel
  Linen 28; matching thread
Purchased overalls with button
  shoulder straps
Tracing paper
7" x 12" piece of coordinating
  fabric for bib back

1 extra button to match those on
  overalls

DIRECTIONS
All seam allowances are ¼".

1. To make bib pattern, first trace outline of cross-stitched design in center of tracing paper. Fold paper in half to find vertical center. Fold overalls in half to find vertical center. Place folded paper on top of overalls, aligning folds. Trace shape of overalls' neckline and top of front shoulder strap onto tracing paper, with top center of traced design 1" below neckline of overalls. Unfold tracing paper. Referring to photo for shape, trace side and bottom edges of bib, coming to a point 2" below bottom center of design. Cut out traced pattern, adding seam allowance to all edges.

2. To make bib, position pattern on design piece, matching traced outline of design to cross-stitched design. Trace pattern. Cut bib front from design piece. Cut bib back from 7" x 12" piece of fabric.

3. With right sides facing and raw edges aligned, stitch bib front to back, leaving a 2″ opening on bottom edge. Trim corners and clip curves. Turn. Slipstitch opening closed. Press. Topstitch around bib close to edge.

4. Position bib on overalls, aligning shoulder straps and necklines; pin in place. Mark placement for buttonholes on bib shoulder straps. Referring to photo, mark third buttonhole ¾″ from center bottom edge. Make buttonholes.

5. Button bib on overalls at shoulders. Mark position for third button and stitch button in place.

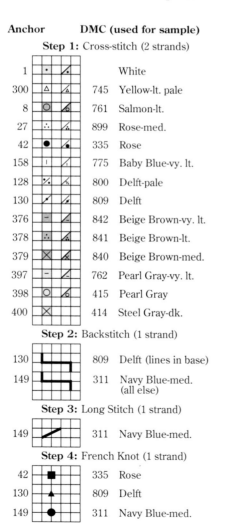

Anchor		DMC (used for sample)	
Step 1: Cross-stitch (2 strands)			
1			White
300		745	Yellow-lt. pale
8		761	Salmon-lt.
27		899	Rose-med.
42		335	Rose
158		775	Baby Blue-vy. lt.
128		800	Delft-pale
130		809	Delft
376		842	Beige Brown-vy. lt.
378		841	Beige Brown-lt.
379		840	Beige Brown-med.
397		762	Pearl Gray-vy. lt.
398		415	Pearl Gray
400		414	Steel Gray-dk.
Step 2: Backstitch (1 strand)			
130		809	Delft (lines in base)
149		311	Navy Blue-med. (all else)
Step 3: Long Stitch (1 strand)			
149		311	Navy Blue-med.
Step 4: French Knot (1 strand)			
42		335	Rose
130		809	Delft
149		311	Navy Blue-med.

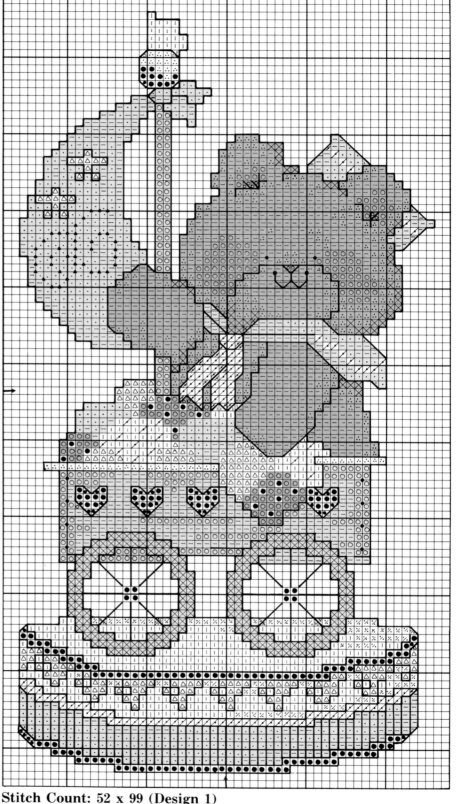

Stitch Count: 52 x 99 (Design 1)

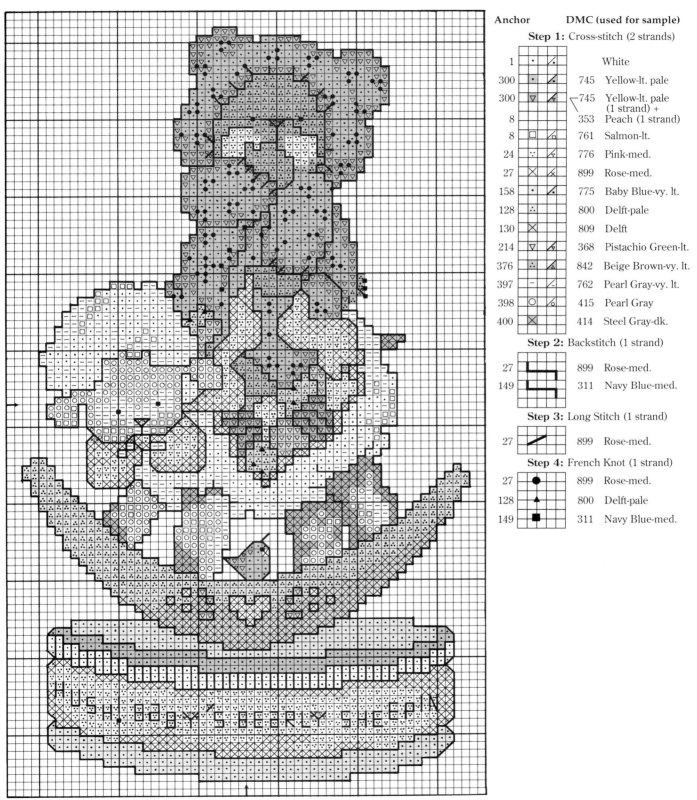

Anchor			DMC (used for sample)	
			Step 1: Cross-stitch (2 strands)	
1	·	⁄		White
300	▨	⁄	745	Yellow-lt. pale
300	▽	⁊	745	Yellow-lt. pale (1 strand) +
8			353	Peach (1 strand)
8	□	⁄	761	Salmon-lt.
24	∴	⁄	776	Pink-med.
27	⊠	⁄	899	Rose-med.
158	·	⁄	775	Baby Blue-vy. lt.
128	∴		800	Delft-pale
130	⊠		809	Delft
214	▽	⁄	368	Pistachio Green-lt.
376	∴	⁄	842	Beige Brown-vy. lt.
397	–	⁄	762	Pearl Gray-vy. lt.
398	○	⁄	415	Pearl Gray
400	⊠		414	Steel Gray-dk.

Step 2: Backstitch (1 strand)

27		899	Rose-med.
149		311	Navy Blue-med.

Step 3: Long Stitch (1 strand)

27	╱	899	Rose-med.

Step 4: French Knot (1 strand)

27	●	899	Rose-med.
128	▲	800	Delft-pale
149	■	311	Navy Blue-med.

Stitch Count: 56 x 98 (Design 2)

81

Wildlife Art Festival

More than 100 painters, print-makers, sculptors, and wood-carvers gather every August in Buckhorn, Ontario, to proudly exhibit their arts and crafts at the Wildlife Art Festival. Join these talented artists and show your skills with this cross-stitched wildlife work of art.

Stitch Count: 137 x 153

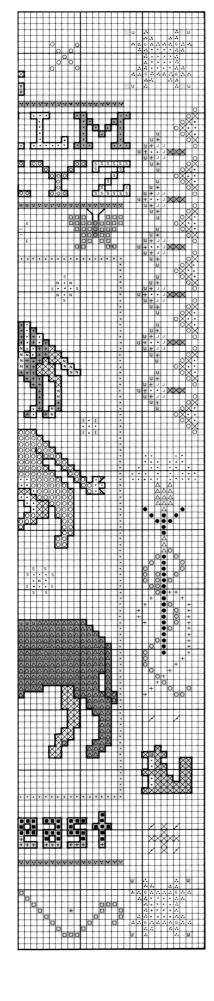

Wildlife Sampler

SAMPLE
Stitched on yellow Glenshee Linen 29 over 2 threads, the finished design size is 9⅜″ x 10½″. The fabric was cut 16″ x 17″.

FABRICS	DESIGN SIZES
Aida 11	12½″ x 13⅞″
Aida 14	9¾″ x 10⅞″
Aida 18	7⅝″ x 8½″
Hardanger 22	6¼″ x 7″

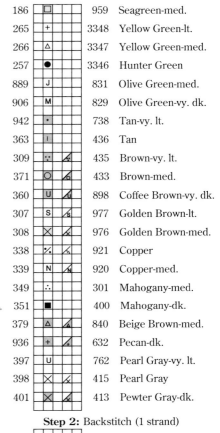

Anchor		DMC (used for sample)	
Step 1: Cross-stitch (2 strands)			
1		White	
300		745	Yellow-lt. pale
301		744	Yellow-pale
891		676	Old Gold-lt.
891 / 398	B	676 / 415	Old Gold-lt. (1 strand) + Pearl Gray (1 strand)
868	−	3779	Terra Cotta-vy. lt.
882	E	407	Pecan
271	+	3713	Salmon-vy. lt.
13	G	347	Salmon-vy. dk.
69	▲	3687	Mauve
897		221	Shell Pink-vy. dk.
95	U	554	Violet-lt.
117	I	341	Blue Violet-lt.
119		3746	Blue Violet-dk.
920	•	932	Antique Blue-lt.
921	△	931	Antique Blue-med.
168	O	807	Peacock Blue
186	□	959	Seagreen-med.
265	+	3348	Yellow Green-lt.
266	△	3347	Yellow Green-med.
257	●	3346	Hunter Green
889	J	831	Olive Green-med.
906	M	829	Olive Green-vy. dk.
942	•	738	Tan-vy. lt.
363	I	436	Tan
309		435	Brown-vy. lt.
371	O	433	Brown-med.
360	U	898	Coffee Brown-vy. dk.
307	S	977	Golden Brown-lt.
308	X	976	Golden Brown-med.
338		921	Copper
339	N	920	Copper-med.
349		301	Mahogany-med.
351	■	400	Mahogany-dk.
379	△	840	Beige Brown-med.
936	+	632	Pecan-dk.
397	U	762	Pearl Gray-vy. lt.
398	X	415	Pearl Gray
401	X	413	Pewter Gray-dk.

Step 2: Backstitch (1 strand)

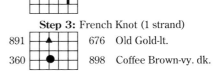

360		898	Coffee Brown-vy. dk.

Step 3: French Knot (1 strand)

891	▲	676	Old Gold-lt.
360	●	898	Coffee Brown-vy. dk.

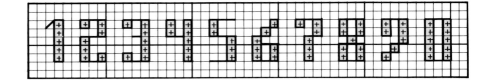

SEPTEMBER
Flower of the Month

Windy, warm days and occasional rain showers combine to make perfect blooming weather for the showy black-eyed Susan, sometimes also called the yellow daisy. These small wildflowers with orange-yellow rays and dark cone-shaped centers tell us that cooler weather is not far away.

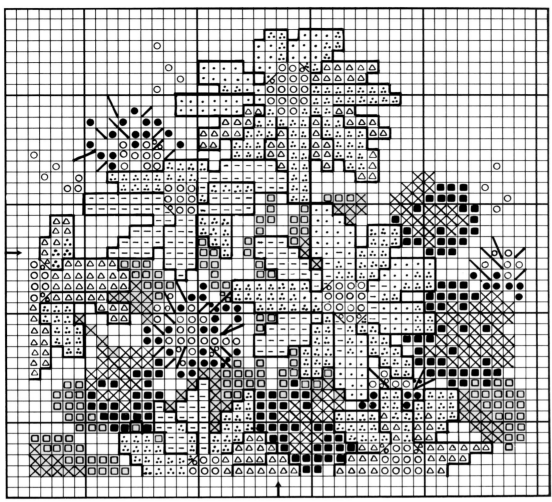

Stitch Count: 44 x 41

Afghan Square: Black-eyed Susans

SAMPLE

Stitched on Vanessa-Ann Afghan Weave 18 over 2 threads, the finished design size is 4⅞″ x 4½″. The fabric was cut 49″ x 59″ for complete afghan. See Suppliers for afghan material. Refer to page 10 for crochet instructions and for diagram showing placement of each design.

FABRICS	DESIGN SIZES
Aida 11	4″ x 3¾″
Aida 14	3⅛″ x 2⅞″
Aida 18	2½″ x 2¼″
Hardanger 22	2″ x 1⅞″

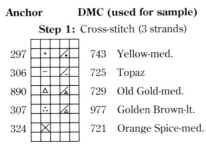

Anchor   **DMC (used for sample)**

Step 1: Cross-stitch (3 strands)

Anchor		DMC	
297	· /	743	Yellow-med.
306	− /	725	Topaz
890	△ /	729	Old Gold-med.
307	∴ /	977	Golden Brown-lt.
324	☒	721	Orange Spice-med.

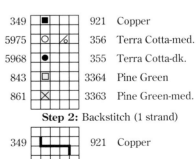

349	■		921	Copper
5975	○ /		356	Terra Cotta-med.
5968	●		355	Terra Cotta-dk.
843	□		3364	Pine Green
861	☒		3363	Pine Green-med.

Step 2: Backstitch (1 strand)

349		921	Copper

Children's Art Festival

As the last days of summer slow-poke into fall, the folks in Doylestown, Pennsylvania, honor their youngest with a children's arts festival. Celebrate the joyful ingenuity of children with this unique piece—designed by a child.

A Child's Creation

SAMPLE
Stitched on khaki Linda 27 over 2 threads, the finished design size for 1 is 7⅞" x 5⅝". The fabric was cut 14" x 12".

FABRICS	DESIGN SIZES
Aida 11	9¾" x 6⅞"
Aida 14	7⅝" x 5½"
Aida 18	6" x 4¼"
Hardanger 22	4⅞" x 3½"

MATERIALS
2 completed cross-stitch designs on khaki Linda 27
1 yard of rust fabric
¼ yard of rust pinstripe fabric
¼ yard of dark brown stripe fabric; matching thread
Scrap of purple fabric
1 (10¾" x 27¾") piece of polyester fleece
Khaki quilting thread

DIRECTIONS
All seam allowances are ¼", except where indicated.

1. With each design centered, trim Linda to 10" x 8". From rust fabric, cut 1 (10¾" x 27¾") piece for backing and 2¼"-wide bias strips, piecing as needed to equal 2½ yards. From rust pinstripe fabric, cut 2 (1¾" x 10") strips and 1 (1½" x 10") strip. From dark brown stripe fabric, cut 4 (1½" x 8") strips and 4 (1½" x 10") strips. From purple fabric, cut 8 (1½") squares.

2. With right sides facing and raw edges aligned, stitch 1 purple square to each end of each 8" dark brown strip. With right sides facing and raw edges aligned, stitch 1 (10") dark brown strip to top and bottom edge of each design piece. Then, with right sides facing and raw edges aligned, stitch 1 brown/purple strip to right and left edges of each design piece.

3. With right sides facing and raw edges aligned, join 1½" and 1¾" rust pinstripe strips and design pieces as shown in Diagram to complete design unit.

4. Stack backing (right side down); fleece; design unit (right side up). Baste together. With khaki thread, quilt near all seams, down center of brown/purple strips, and near edge of cross-stitched design. Trim fleece from seam. Trim backing to match top.

5. Using ½" seam, bind edges with bias strips, mitering corners.

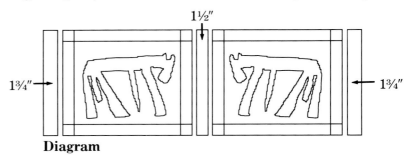

Diagram

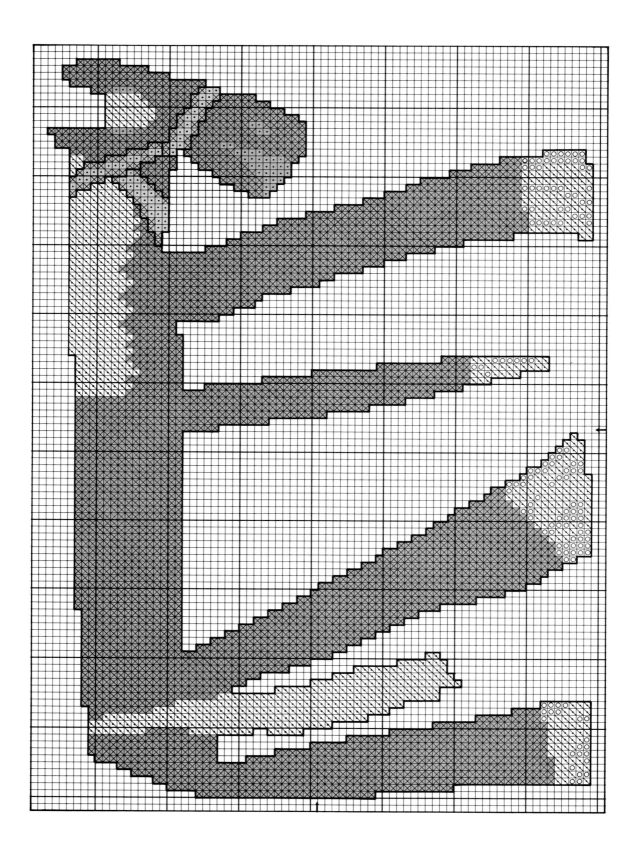

Stitch Count: 107 x 76 (for 1)

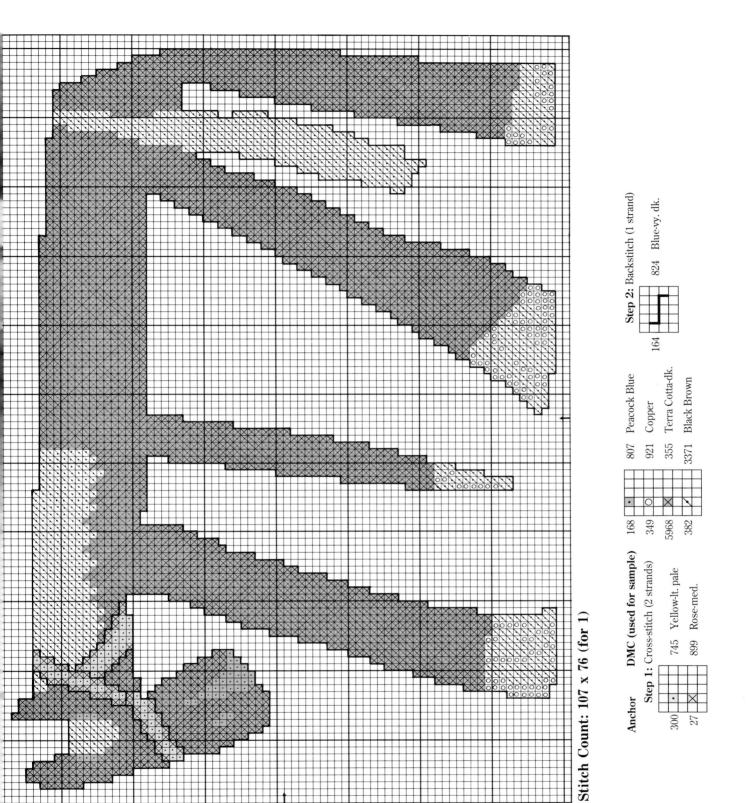

Anchor	DMC (used for sample)		
	Step 1: Cross-stitch (2 strands)		
300	745	Yellow-lt. pale	
27	899	Rose-med.	
168	807	Peacock Blue	
349	921	Copper	
5968	355	Terra Cotta-dk.	
382	3371	Black Brown	
	Step 2: Backstitch (1 strand)		
164	824	Blue-vy. dk.	

OCTOBER
Flower of the Month

In fall, the green leaves of summer have turned to brilliant shades of gold, orange, and red. October means leaves blowing in your face as you walk, leaves under the feet of trick-or-treaters, and leaves to rake on Saturday afternoon.

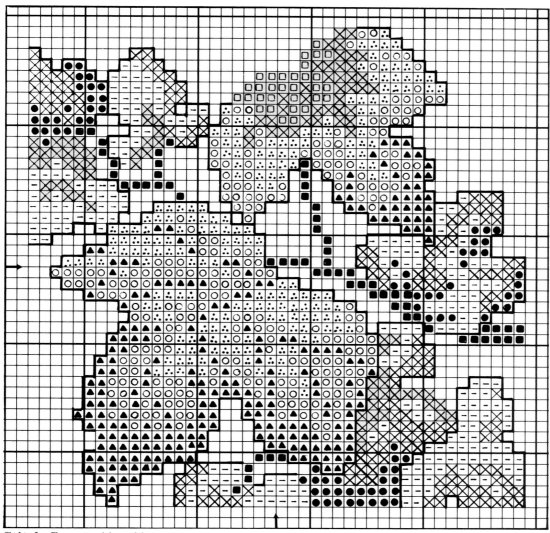

Stitch Count: 44 x 44

Afghan Square: Leaves

SAMPLE

Stitched on Vanessa-Ann Afghan Weave 18 over 2 threads, the finished design size is 4⅞″ x 4⅞″. The fabric was cut 49″ x 59″ for complete afghan. See Suppliers for afghan material. Refer to page 10 for crochet instructions and for diagram showing placement of each design.

FABRICS	DESIGN SIZES
Aida 11	4″ x 4″
Aida 14	3⅛″ x 3⅛″
Aida 18	2½″ x 2½″
Hardanger 22	2″ x 2″

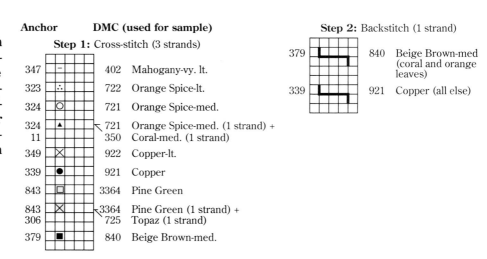

Anchor		DMC (used for sample)	
	Step 1: Cross-stitch (3 strands)		
347	−	402	Mahogany-vy. lt.
323	∴	722	Orange Spice-lt.
324	O	721	Orange Spice-med.
324 11	▲	721 350	Orange Spice-med. (1 strand) + Coral-med. (1 strand)
349	✕	922	Copper-lt.
339	●	921	Copper
843	▫	3364	Pine Green
843 306	✕	3364 725	Pine Green (1 strand) + Topaz (1 strand)
379	■	840	Beige Brown-med.

Step 2: Backstitch (1 strand)

379		840	Beige Brown-med (coral and orange leaves)
339		921	Copper (all else)

OCTOBER
Octoberfest

The harvest is in. The pantry is full. The days are getting cooler, and the leaves are turning a bright gold and orange. Fall is in the air, and with fall comes Octoberfest—a family time of entertainment, food, and arts and crafts. And this year, with five weekends in October, there will be an extra weekend for these special celebrations.

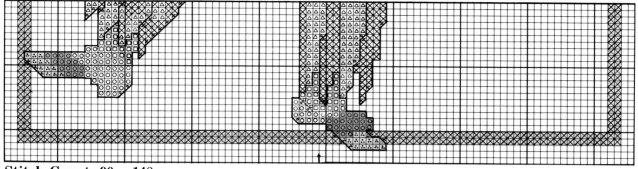

Stitch Count: 90 x 148

Fall Harvest Banners

SAMPLE for Man Banner
Stitched on black Damask Aida 14
over 1 thread, the finished design
size is 6⅜" x 10⅝". The fabric was
cut 10" x 18".

FABRICS	DESIGN SIZES
Aida 11	8⅛" x 13½"
Aida 14	6⅜" x 10⅝"
Aida 18	5" x 8¼"
Hardanger 22	4⅛" x 6¾"

SAMPLE for Woman Banner
Stitched on black Damask Aida 14
over 1 thread, the finished design
size is 6¾" x 10⅝". The fabric was
cut 10" x 18".

FABRICS	DESIGN SIZES
Aida 11	8⅝" x 13½"
Aida 14	6¾" x 10⅝"
Aida 18	5¼" x 8¼"
Hardanger 22	4⅜" x 6¾"

MATERIALS (for 1 banner)
Completed cross-stitch on black
  Damask Aida 14; matching
  thread
½ yard of unstitched black Damask Aida 14
⅓ yard of olive green satin
  fabric
1½ yards (⅛") cording
Batting

DIRECTIONS
All seam allowances are ¼".

1. With design centered, trim
Damask to 9" x 16¼". From unstitched Damask, cut 1 (9" x 16¼")
piece for back and 3 (2½" x 3½")
pieces for tabs. From batting, cut
1 (9" x 16¼") piece. From satin, cut
1"-wide bias strips, piecing as
needed to equal 51". Make corded
piping.

2. To attach piping, with right
sides facing and raw edges aligned,
stitch piping around all sides of
design piece.

3. To make tabs, with right sides
facing and raw edges aligned, fold
each tab piece in half lengthwise.
Stitch long edges of each tab piece
together, leaving ends open. Turn.
Fold each tab in half, matching
ends; baste. To attach tabs, with
right sides facing and raw edges
aligned, pin 1 tab to top center of
design piece. Pin second tab 1½" to
left of center tab and remaining
tab 1½" to right.

4. Stack batting, backing (right
side up), and design piece (right
side down). Stitch together
through all layers, sewing along
stitching line of piping and leaving
an opening for turning. Trim batting from seam allowance. Clip
corners and turn. Slipstitch opening closed.

Anchor	DMC (used for sample)	
Step 1: Cross-stitch (2 strands)		
1		White
886	677	Old Gold-vy. lt.
891	676	Old Gold-lt.
890	729	Old Gold-med.
373	3045	Yellow Beige-dk.
306	725	Topaz
323	722	Orange Spice-lt.
324	721	Orange Spice-med.
326	720	Orange Spice-dk.
339	920	Copper-med.
5975	356	Terra Cotta-med.
10	3328	Salmon-dk.
11	350	Coral-med.
13	347	Salmon-vy. dk.
970	315	Antique Mauve-vy. dk.
846	3051	Green Gray-dk.
874	833	Olive Green-lt.
889	830	Olive Green-dk.
363	436	Tan
360	898	Coffee Brown-vy. dk.
Step 2: Backstitch (1 strand)		
13	347	Salmon-vy. dk. (radishes)
889	830	Olive Green-dk. (stems at top of hat)
360	898	Coffee Brown-vy. dk. (all else)

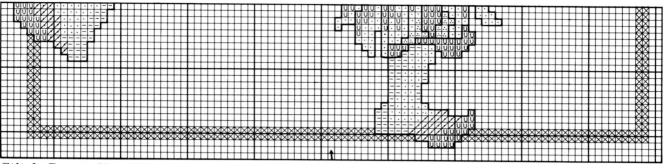

Stitch Count: 95 x 148

Anchor	DMC (used for sample)	
Step 1: Cross-stitch (2 strands)		

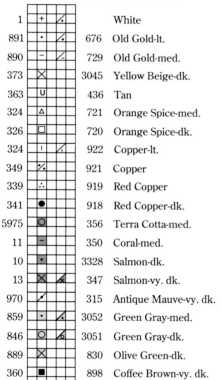

Anchor		DMC	
1	+ ⟋		White
891	· ⟋	676	Old Gold-lt.
890	= ⟋	729	Old Gold-med.
373	✕	3045	Yellow Beige-dk.
363	U	436	Tan
324	△	721	Orange Spice-med.
326	▢	720	Orange Spice-dk.
324	ı ⟋	922	Copper-lt.
349	⁒	921	Copper
339	∴	919	Red Copper
341	●	918	Red Copper-dk.
5975	◯	356	Terra Cotta-med.
11	▬	350	Coral-med.
10	▪	3328	Salmon-dk.
13	✕ ◿	347	Salmon-vy. dk.
970	⟋	315	Antique Mauve-vy. dk.
859	· ⟋	3052	Green Gray-med.
846	◯ ◿	3051	Green Gray-dk.
889	✕	830	Olive Green-dk.
360	■	898	Coffee Brown-vy. dk.

Step 2: Backstitch (1 strand)

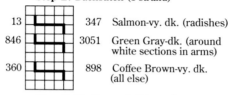

13	347	Salmon-vy. dk. (radishes)
846	3051	Green Gray-dk. (around white sections in arms)
360	898	Coffee Brown-vy. dk. (all else)

Step 3: Feather and ribbon placement

●	Feather
▲	Ribbon

OCTOBER 12
Columbus Day 500th Anniversary

This day marks the quincentenary of the discovery of America by Christopher Columbus in 1492. After a long voyage beginning in Palos, Spain, and sailing through the Canary Islands, Columbus sighted land. He went ashore on San Salvador, which is now called Watlings Island, in the Bahamas. This year, while celebrations of the event take place around the country, you can join in with this cross-stitched version of an ancient wall map.

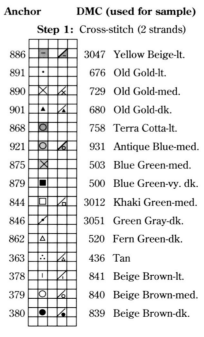

Ancient Wall Map

SAMPLE

Stitched on driftwood Belfast
Linen 32 over 2 threads, the fin-
ished design size is 15⅝″ x 11¼″.
The fabric was cut 22″ x 18″.

FABRICS	DESIGN SIZES
Aida 11	22⅞″ x 16⅜″
Aida 14	17⅞″ x 12⅞″
Aida 18	14″ x 10″
Hardanger 22	11⅜″ x 8⅛″

Anchor			DMC (used for sample)	
Step 1: Cross-stitch (2 strands)				
886	▬	◿	3047	Yellow Beige-lt.
891	·		676	Old Gold-lt.
890	✕	◪	729	Old Gold-med.
901	▲	◿	680	Old Gold-dk.
868	◯		758	Terra Cotta-lt.
921	◎	◿	931	Antique Blue-med.
875	✕		503	Blue Green-med.
879	■		500	Blue Green-vy. dk.
844	☐	◿	3012	Khaki Green-med.
846	╱		3051	Green Gray-dk.
862	△		520	Fern Green-dk.
363	∴	◿	436	Tan
378	I	╱	841	Beige Brown-lt.
379	◯	◪	840	Beige Brown-med.
380	●	◿	839	Beige Brown-dk.

Step 2: Backstitch (1 strand)

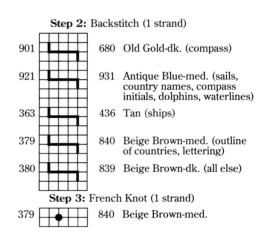

901	680	Old Gold-dk. (compass)
921	931	Antique Blue-med. (sails, country names, compass initials, dolphins, waterlines)
363	436	Tan (ships)
379	840	Beige Brown-med. (outline of countries, lettering)
380	839	Beige Brown-dk. (all else)

Step 3: French Knot (1 strand)

379	840	Beige Brown-med.

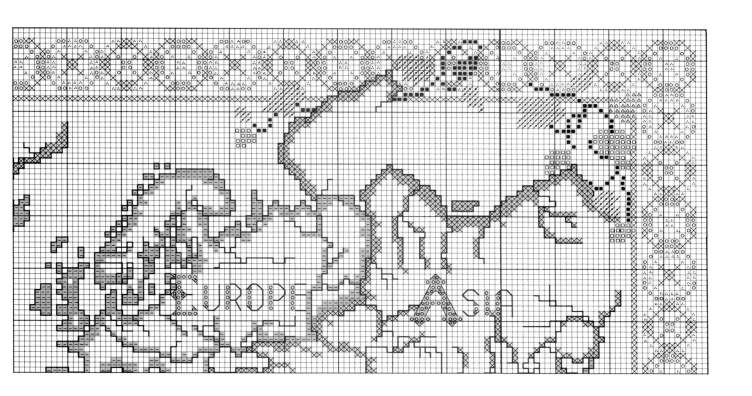

Stitch Count: 251 x 180

NOVEMBER
Flower of the Month

Chrysanthemums, which usually appear in autumn, are known for their abundant blossoms. The flowers are very adaptable, having a wide range of both color and size. The large individual mums are often used to make the beautiful homecoming corsages worn at football games.

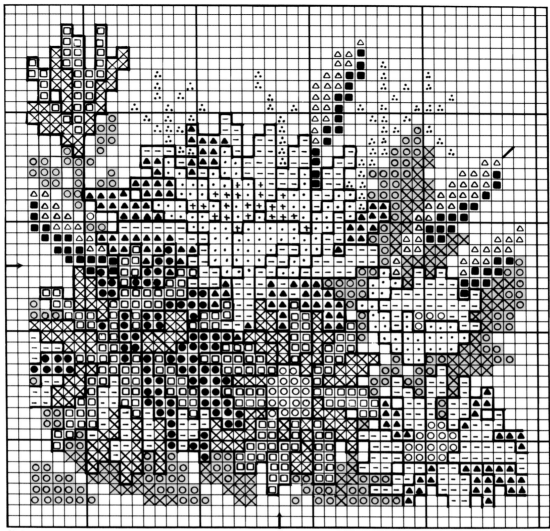

Stitch Count: 44 x 44

Afghan Square: Chrysanthemums

SAMPLE

Stitched on Vanessa-Ann Afghan Weave 18 over 2 threads, the finished design size is 4⅞″ x 4⅞″. The fabric was cut 49″ x 59″ for complete afghan. See Suppliers for afghan material. Refer to page 10 for crochet instructions and for diagram showing placement of each design.

FABRICS
Aida 11
Aida 14
Aida 18
Hardanger 22

DESIGN SIZES
4″ x 4″
3⅛″ x 3⅛″
2½″ x 2½″
2″ x 2″

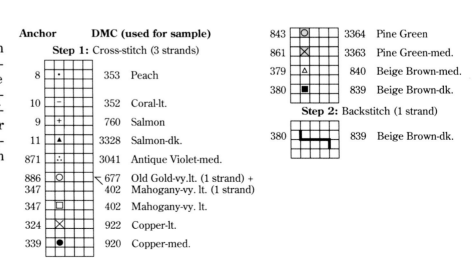

Anchor		DMC (used for sample)	
		Step 1: Cross-stitch (3 strands)	
8	·	353	Peach
10	−	352	Coral-lt.
9	+	760	Salmon
11	▲	3328	Salmon-dk.
871	∴	3041	Antique Violet-med.
886	◯	677	Old Gold-vy.lt. (1 strand) +
347		402	Mahogany-vy. lt. (1 strand)
347	☐	402	Mahogany-vy. lt.
324	✕	922	Copper-lt.
339	●	920	Copper-med.
843	◯	3364	Pine Green
861	✕	3363	Pine Green-med.
379	△	840	Beige Brown-med.
380	■	839	Beige Brown-dk.
		Step 2: Backstitch (1 strand)	
380		839	Beige Brown-dk.

NOVEMBER 26
Thanksgiving

In 1863, President Abraham Lincoln proclaimed Thanksgiving a national holiday. This serving tray would fit right into the Victorian styling of that era. Cross-stitch the ornate floral design here to make an elegant tray for Thanksgiving.

Victorian Serving Tray

SAMPLE

Stitched on dirty linen Dublin Linen 25 over 2 threads, the finished design size is 12⅜″ x 22½″. The fabric was cut 19″ x 29″. To complete project, place design piece in an antique serving tray and cover it with glass.

FABRICS	DESIGN SIZES
Aida 11	14⅛″ x 25½″
Aida 14	11⅛″ x 20⅛″
Aida 18	8⅝″ x 15⅝″
Hardanger 22	7″ x 12¾″

Anchor **DMC (used for sample)**

Step 1: Cross-stitch (2 strands)

Anchor		DMC	
293	□	727	Topaz-vy. lt.
295	R	726	Topaz-lt.
306	◆	725	Topaz
891		676	Old Gold-lt.
366	·	951	Peach Pecan-lt.
323	N	722	Orange Spice-lt.
868	∕	3779	Terra Cotta-vy. lt.
914		3064	Pecan-lt.
11	·	3328	Salmon-dk.
13	X	347	Salmon-vy. dk.
271	–	3713	Salmon-vy. lt.

Anchor		DMC	
50	O	3716	Wild Rose-lt.
76	∵	961	Wild Rose-dk.
897	△	221	Shell Pink-vy. dk.
95	–	554	Violet-lt.
98	△	553	Violet-med.
99	∴	552	Violet-dk.
130	·	809	Delft
131	O	798	Delft-dk.
133	X	796	Royal Blue-dk.
255	+	907	Parrot Green-lt.
256	U	906	Parrot Green-med.
258	▲	904	Parrot Green-vy. dk.
214	◇	368	Pistachio Green-lt.
215	⁒	320	Pistachio Green-med.
268	P	3345	Hunter Green-dk.
246	◪	319	Pistachio Green-vy. dk.
879	●	890	Pistachio Green-ultra dk.
898	◙	611	Drab Brown-dk.
905	W	3031	Mocha Brown-vy. dk.
397	I	3072	Beaver Gray-vy. lt.
900	‹	647	Beaver Gray-med.
8581	╱	646	Beaver Gray-dk.
401	■	844	Beaver Gray-ultra dk.

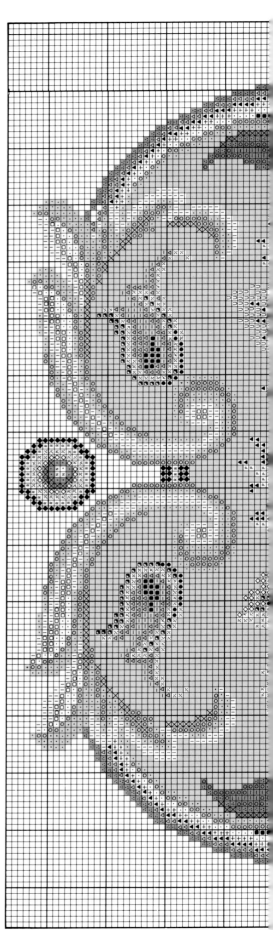

Stitch Count: 155 x 281

DECEMBER
Flower of the Month

The poinsettia was named after Joel Roberts Poinsett, U.S. minister to Mexico from 1825-1829. He fell in love with this Mexican plant and introduced it to his garden in Charleston, South Carolina. It soon became a favorite holiday decoration.

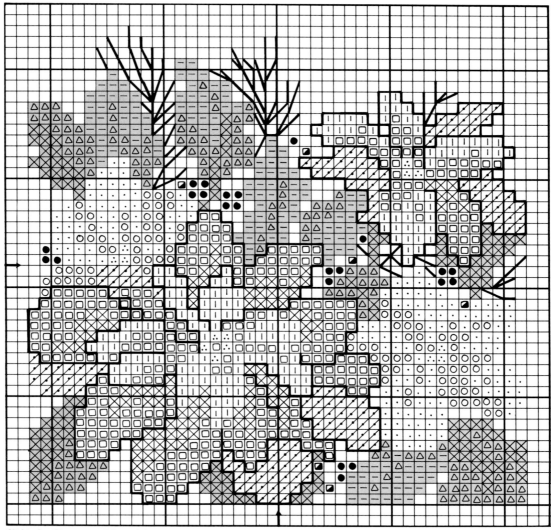

Stitch Count: 44 x 44

Afghan Square: Poinsettias

SAMPLE
Stitched on Vanessa-Ann Afghan Weave 18 over 2 threads, the finished design size is 4⅞″ x 4⅞″. The fabric was cut 49″ x 59″ for complete afghan. See Suppliers for afghan material. Refer to page 10 for crochet instructions and for diagram showing placement of each design.

FABRICS
Aida 11
Aida 14
Aida 18
Hardanger 22

DESIGN SIZES
4″ x 4″
3⅛″ x 3⅛″
2½″ x 2½″
2″ x 2″

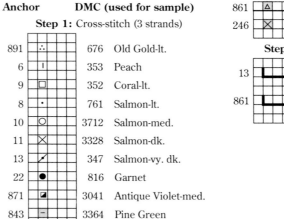

Anchor		DMC (used for sample)	
		Step 1: Cross-stitch (3 strands)	
891	∴	676	Old Gold-lt.
6	I	353	Peach
9	□	352	Coral-lt.
8	·	761	Salmon-lt.
10	○	3712	Salmon-med.
11	X	3328	Salmon-dk.
13	╱	347	Salmon-vy. dk.
22	●	816	Garnet
871	◪	3041	Antique Violet-med.
843	—	3364	Pine Green

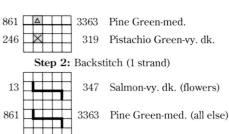

861	△	3363	Pine Green-med.
246	X	319	Pistachio Green-vy. dk.

Step 2: Backstitch (1 strand)

13		347	Salmon-vy. dk. (flowers)
861		3363	Pine Green-med. (all else)

DECEMBER 9
Legendary Christmas

Renewing the celebrations of years past often creates a powerful nostalgia. That's the spirit that the people of Chesterfield, Virginia, capture each year when they gather for their Legendary Christmas. It's also the spirit captured by this medieval cross-stitched piece.

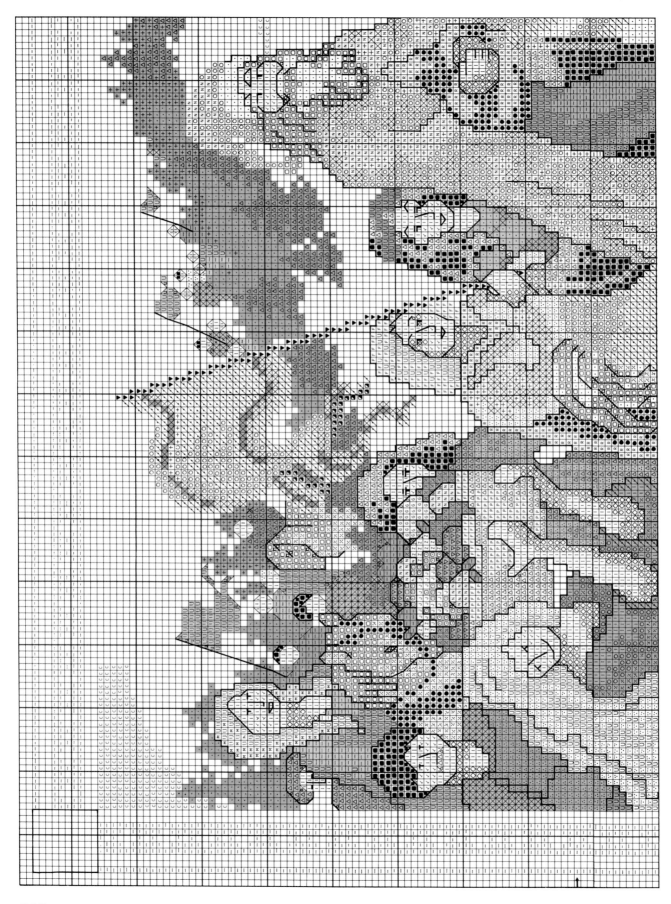

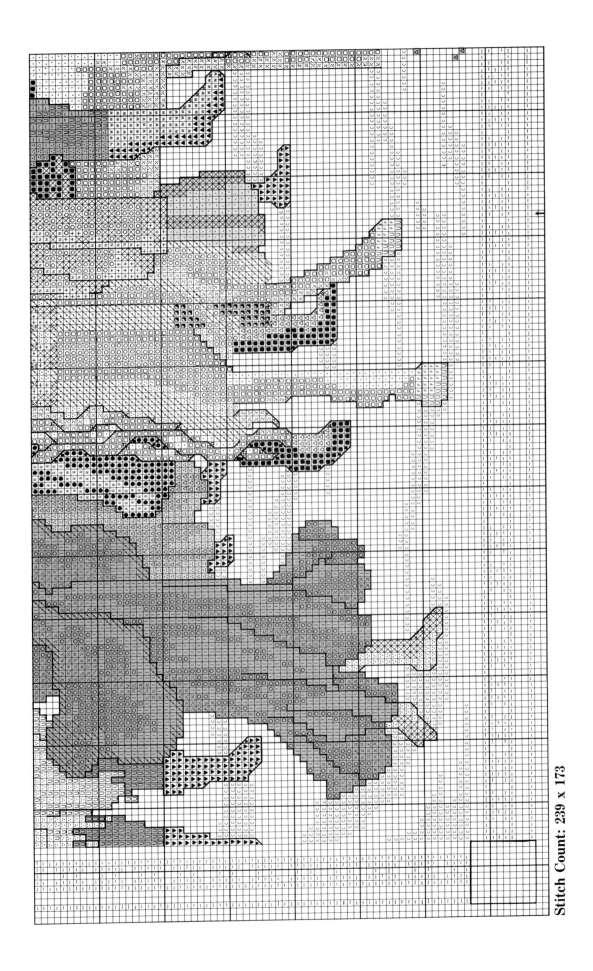

Stitch Count: 239 x 173

Medieval Christmas Parade

SAMPLE
Stitched on white Belfast Linen 32 over 2 threads, the finished design size is 14⅞" x 10¾". The fabric was cut 21" x 17".

FABRICS	DESIGN SIZES
Aida 11	21¾" x 15¾"
Aida 14	17⅛" x 12⅜"
Aida 18	13¼" x 9⅝"
Hardanger 22	10⅞" x 7⅞"

Anchor	Symbol	DMC	Color
1	·		White
306	Z	725	Topaz
306	+	725	Topaz (2 strands) + Gold Metalic (1 strand)
890	X	729	Old Gold-med.
901	∴	680	Old Gold-dk.
880	–	948	Peach-vy. lt.
881	‹	754	Peach-lt.
4146	◇	950	Peach Pecan-dk.
323	G	722	Orange Spice-lt.
9	▽	352	Coral-lt.
10	–	3712	Salmon-med.
11	U	3328	Salmon-dk.
341	▶	3777	Terra Cotta-vy. dk.
896	R	3722	Shell Pink
19	N	817	Coral Red-vy. dk.
20	○	498	Christmas Red-dk.
43	◹	815	Garnet-med.
44	◣	814	Garnet-dk.
72	●	902	Garnet-vy. dk.
968	◩	778	Antique Mauve-vy. lt.
870	–	3042	Antique Violet-lt.
871	○	3041	Antique Violet-med.
872	⊠	3740	Antique Violet-dk.
168	◁	807	Peacock Blue
169	∴	806	Peacock Blue-dk.
920	·	932	Antique Blue-lt.
921	+	931	Antique Blue-med.
922	X	930	Antique Blue-dk.
849	–	927	Slate Green-med.
849	C	927	Slate Green-med. (1 strand)

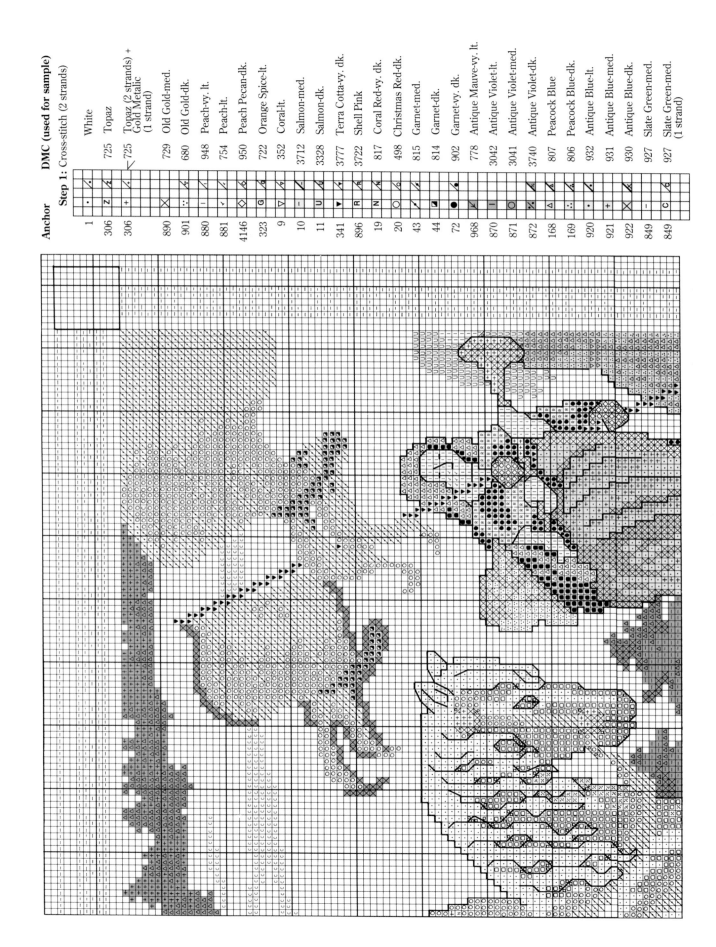

Symbol	DMC	Anchor	Color
J	472	264	Avocado Green-ultra lt.
⊡	989	242	Forest Green
│	562	210	Jade-med.
U	561	212	Jade-vy. dk.
+	503	875	Blue Green-med. (1 strand)
·	503	875	Blue Green-med.
◩	502	876	Blue Green
☒	501	878	Blue Green-dk.
∴	500	879	Blue Green-vy. dk.
F	437	362	Tan-lt.
U	435	309	Brown-vy. lt.
M	433	371	Brown-med.
P	840	379	Beige Brown-med.
◁	839	380	Beige Brown-dk.
■	838	381	Beige Brown-vy. dk.
◱	762	397	Pearl Gray-vy. lt.
□	453	399	Shell Gray-lt.
⋰	317	400	Pewter Gray
W	3799	236	Pewter Gray-vy. dk.

Step 2: Backstitch (1 strand)

DMC	Anchor	Color
927	849	Slate Green-med. (border)
840	379	Beige Brown-med. (faces)
317	400	Pewter Gray (horses and Santa's beard)
838	381	Beige Brown-vy. dk. (all else)

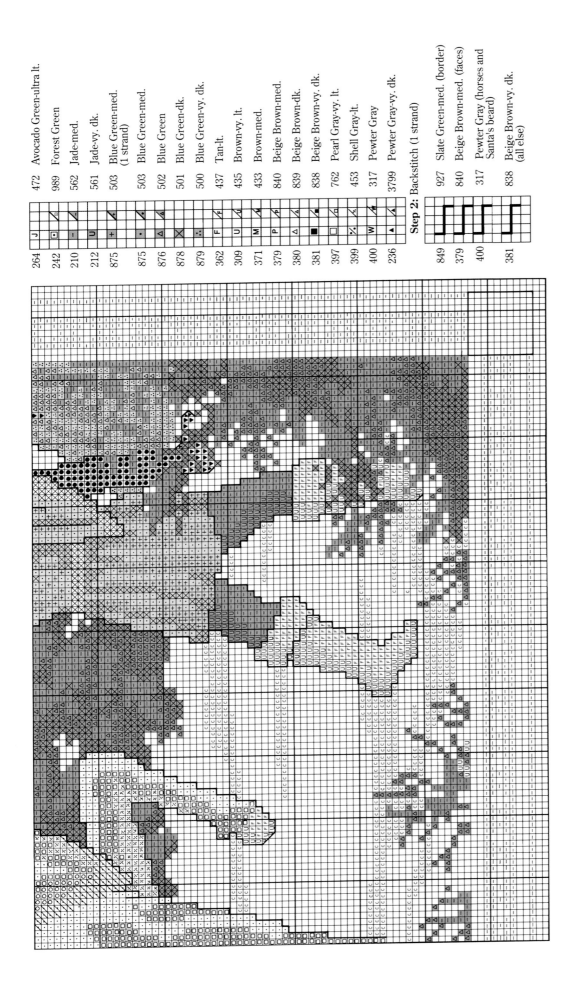

DECEMBER 24
Christmas Eve

Decorating the house for the holidays is a favorite tradition that everyone enjoys. And one of the prettiest decorations is the poinsettia, which has been considered the Christmas flower since the 17th century. The star-shaped flower is most commonly thought of as being a deep red, but white, pink, and yellow varieties are also popular. These lovely cross-stitched pieces embellished with poinsettias will add charm to your holiday decorating.

Christmas Ensemble

SAMPLE for Cornucopia
Stitched on ivory Linda 27 over 2 threads, finished design size is 7⅞″ x 2¾″. Fabric was cut 14″ x 9″.

FABRICS	DESIGN SIZES
Aida 11	9⅝″ x 3⅜″
Aida 14	7⅝″ x 2⅝″
Aida 18	5⅞″ x 2″
Hardanger 22	4⅞″ x 1⅝″

MATERIALS for Cornucopia
Completed cross-stitch on ivory Linda 27; matching thread
¼ yard of light peach satin
4¾ yards (1/16″-wide) peach satin ribbon
¼ yard of heavyweight fusible interfacing
⅓ yard (⅛″) cording
Tracing paper
Dressmakers' pen

DIRECTIONS
The pattern includes ¼″ seam allowance.

1. Make pattern. Place pattern on design piece with top edge of pattern 1″ above and parallel to top row of stitching. Cut out.

2. From interfacing, cut 1 piece the same size as design piece. From satin, cut 1 lining piece. Also, cut 1″-wide bias strips, piecing as needed to equal ⅓ yard. Make corded piping.

3. From ribbon, cut 6 (12″) pieces for bows and 4 (24″) pieces for hanger.

4. Following manufacturer's instructions, fuse interfacing to wrong side of design piece.

5. To attach piping, with right sides facing and raw edges aligned, stitch piping along top edge of design piece. With right sides facing and raw edges aligned, fold design piece in half and stitch along straight edge (back seam). Turn.

6. With right sides facing and raw edges aligned, fold lining in half and stitch along straight edge (back seam), leaving an opening for turning. Do not turn. With right sides facing and seams matching, slide lining over cornucopia. Stitch around top edge of cornucopia, sewing along stitching line of piping. Turn through opening. Slipstitch opening closed. Tuck lining inside cornucopia.

7. Handling 3 (12″) pieces of ribbon as 1, tie a bow. Repeat with remaining 12″ pieces. With seam centered in back, tack bows to top of cornucopia on opposite sides.

8. To make hanger, handling 2 (24″) pieces of ribbon as 1, fold ribbons in half. Tack fold on inside edge opposite bow. Repeat on other side. Knot all ends together.

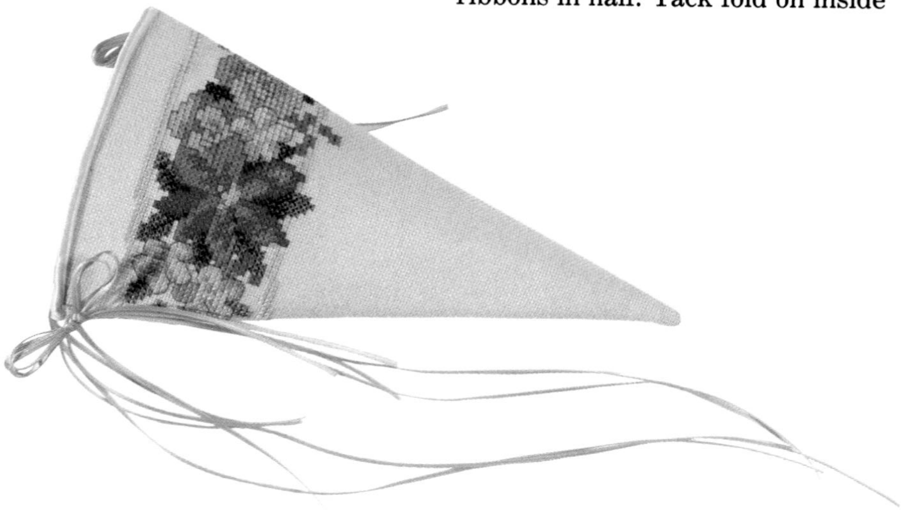

SAMPLE for Stocking Ornament
Stitched on ivory Linda 27 over 2 threads, finished design size is 2⅞″ x 4¼″. Fabric was cut 9″ x 10″.

FABRICS	DESIGN SIZES
Aida 11	3½″ x 5¼″
Aida 14	2¾″ x 4⅛″
Aida 18	2⅛″ x 3¼″
Hardanger 22	1¾″ x 2⅝″

MATERIALS for Stocking Ornament
Completed cross-stitch on ivory Linda 27; matching thread
Scrap of unstitched ivory Linda 27 for back
½ yard of light peach satin
⅓ yard (1/16″-wide) peach satin ribbon
½ yard (⅛″) cording
Tracing paper
Dressmakers' pen

DIRECTIONS
The pattern includes ¼″ seam allowance.

1. Make pattern. Center pattern on design piece and cut out.

2. From unstitched Linda, cut 1 stocking piece for back.

3. From satin, cut 2 stocking pieces for lining and 1″-wide bias strips, piecing as needed to equal ½ yard. Make corded piping. Cut piping into 1 (12″) and 1 (6″) piece.

4. To attach piping, with right sides facing and raw edges aligned, stitch 30″ piece of piping around sides and bottom of stocking front. With right sides facing, stitch stocking front to stocking back, sewing along the stitching line of piping and leaving top open. Clip curves. Turn. With right sides facing and raw edges aligned, stitch remaining piping around top of stocking.

5. To make stocking lining, with right sides facing and raw edges aligned, stitch together lining front and back, leaving top edge open and a large opening in side seam above heel. Clip curves. Do not turn. With right sides facing, slide lining over stocking, matching side seams. Stitch lining to stocking around top edge, sewing along stitching line of piping. Turn stocking through opening in lining. Slipstitch opening closed. Tuck lining inside stocking.

6. To make hanger, fold 10″ ribbon in half to form a loop. Tack ends of ribbon to ornament back at top left corner.

SAMPLE for Heart Ornament
Stitched on ivory Linda 27 over 2 threads, finished design size is 3¼″ x 2⅞″. Fabric was cut 10″ x 9″.

FABRICS	DESIGN SIZES
Aida 11	4″ x 3½″
Aida 14	3⅛″ x 2¾″
Aida 18	2½″ x 2⅛″
Hardanger 22	2″ x 1¾″

SAMPLE for Bell Ornament
Stitched on ivory Linda 27 over 2 threads, finished design size is 2¼″ x 3⅛″. Fabric was cut 9″ x 9″.

FABRICS	DESIGN SIZES
Aida 11	2¾″ x 3⅞″
Aida 14	2⅛″ x 3″
Aida 18	1⅝″ x 2⅜″
Hardanger 22	1⅜″ x 1⅞″

MATERIALS for Heart or Bell Ornament
Completed cross-stitch on ivory Linda 27; matching thread

Scrap of unstitched ivory Linda 27 for back
¼ yard of light peach satin
⅓ yard (1⁄16″-wide) peach satin ribbon
⅓ yard (⅛″) cording
Stuffing
Tracing paper
Dressmakers' pen

DIRECTIONS
The patterns include ¼″ seam allowances.

1. Make pattern. Center pattern on design piece and cut out.

2. From unstitched Linda, cut 1 piece for back.

3. From satin, cut 1″-wide bias strips, piecing as needed to equal ⅓ yard. Make corded piping.

4. To attach piping, with right sides facing and raw edges aligned, stitch piping around edges of design piece.

5. With right sides facing, stitch front to back, leaving an opening for turning. Clip curves. Turn. Stuff moderately. Slipstitch opening closed.

6. To make hanger, fold 10″ ribbon in half to form a loop. Tack ends of ribbon to ornament back at top center.

SAMPLE for Stocking
Stitched on ivory Linda 27 over 2 threads, the finished design size is 7¼″ x 11⅞″. The fabric was cut 14″ x 18″.

FABRICS	DESIGN SIZES
Aida 11	8⅞″ x 14½″
Aida 14	7″ x 11⅜″
Aida 18	5⅛″ x 8⅞″
Hardanger 22	4½″ x 7¼″

MATERIALS for Stocking
Completed cross-stitch on ivory Linda 27; matching thread
½ yard of unstitched ivory Linda 27 for stocking back
1 yard of light peach satin
1¼ yards (⅛″) cording
Tracing paper
Dressmakers' pen

DIRECTIONS
The pattern includes ¼″ seam allowance.

1. Make pattern. For stocking front, place pattern on design piece with top edge of pattern ¼″ above and parallel to top row of stitching. Cut out.

2. From unstitched Linda, cut 1 stocking piece for back.

3. From satin, cut 2 stocking pieces for lining and 1 (2½″ x 3½″) strip for hanger. Also, cut 1″-wide bias strips, piecing as needed to equal 1¼ yards. Make corded piping. Cut piping into 1 (30″) and 1 (13″) piece.

4. With right sides facing and raw edges aligned, fold hanger in half lengthwise. Stitch long raw edge and turn. With raw edges aligned, fold hanger in half; press.

5. To attach piping, refer to step 4 of Stocking Ornament. With raw edges aligned, baste ends of hanger to top left-hand edge of stocking back.

6. To make lining, refer to step 5 of Stocking Ornament.

See page 128 for patterns.

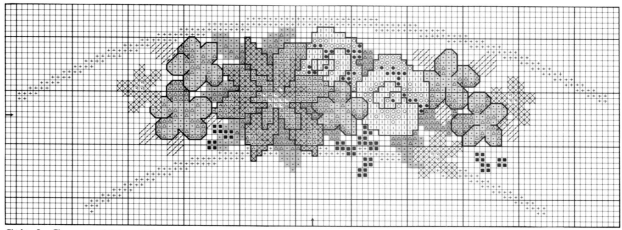

**Stitch Count: 106 x 37
(Cornucopia)**

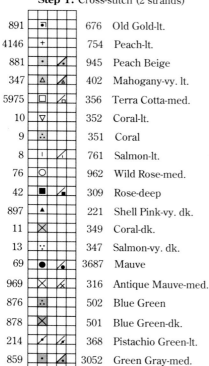

Anchor		DMC (used for sample)	
Step 1: Cross-stitch (2 strands)			
891	⊡	676	Old Gold-lt.
4146	+	754	Peach-lt.
881	· ◹	945	Peach Beige
347	△ ◩	402	Mahogany-vy. lt.
5975	☐ ◿	356	Terra Cotta-med.
10	▽	352	Coral-lt.
9	∴	351	Coral
8	╎ ╱	761	Salmon-lt.
76	○	962	Wild Rose-med.
42	■ ◪	309	Rose-deep
897	▲	221	Shell Pink-vy. dk.
11	✕	349	Coral-dk.
13	∴	347	Salmon-vy. dk.
69	● ◿	3687	Mauve
969	✕ ╳	316	Antique Mauve-med.
876	∷	502	Blue Green
878	✕	501	Blue Green-dk.
214	╱ ◿	368	Pistachio Green-lt.
859	· ◢	3052	Green Gray-med.
846	△ ◩	3051	Green Gray-dk.

Step 2: Backstitch (1 strand)

Anchor		DMC	
347		402	Mahogany-vy. lt. (beige flowers)
69		3687	Mauve (pink flowers, peach flowers on bell)
897		221	Shell Pink-vy. dk. (dark poinsettias)
42		309	Rose-deep (lattice work; toe, heel, top of stocking)
11		349	Coral-dk. (all else)

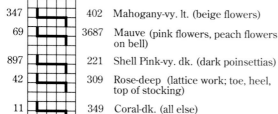

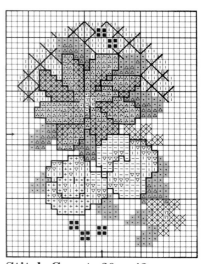

**Stitch Count: 39 x 58
(Stocking Ornament)**

**Stitch Count: 30 x 42
(Bell Ornament)**

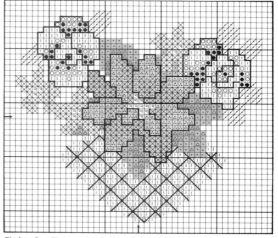

Stitch Count: 44 x 39 (Heart Ornament)

126

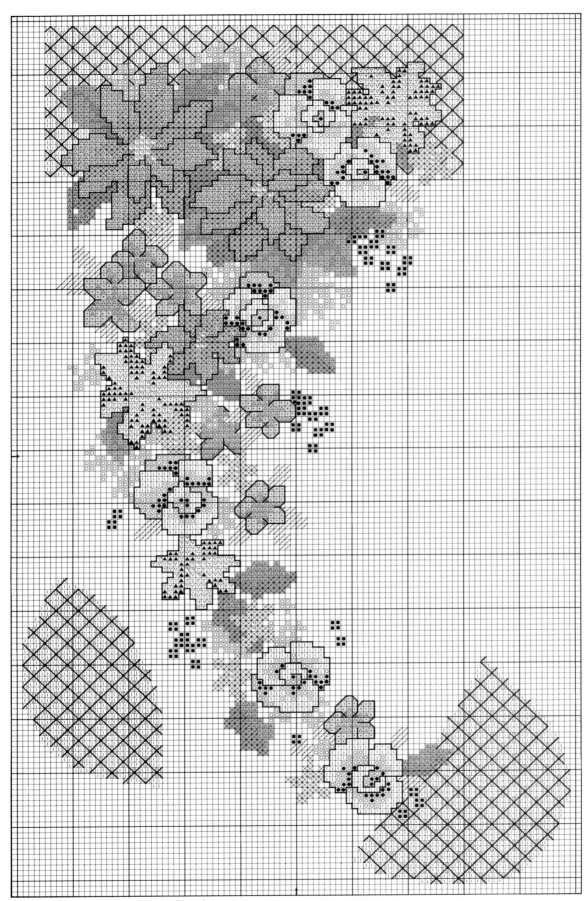

Stitch Count: 98 x 160 (Stocking)

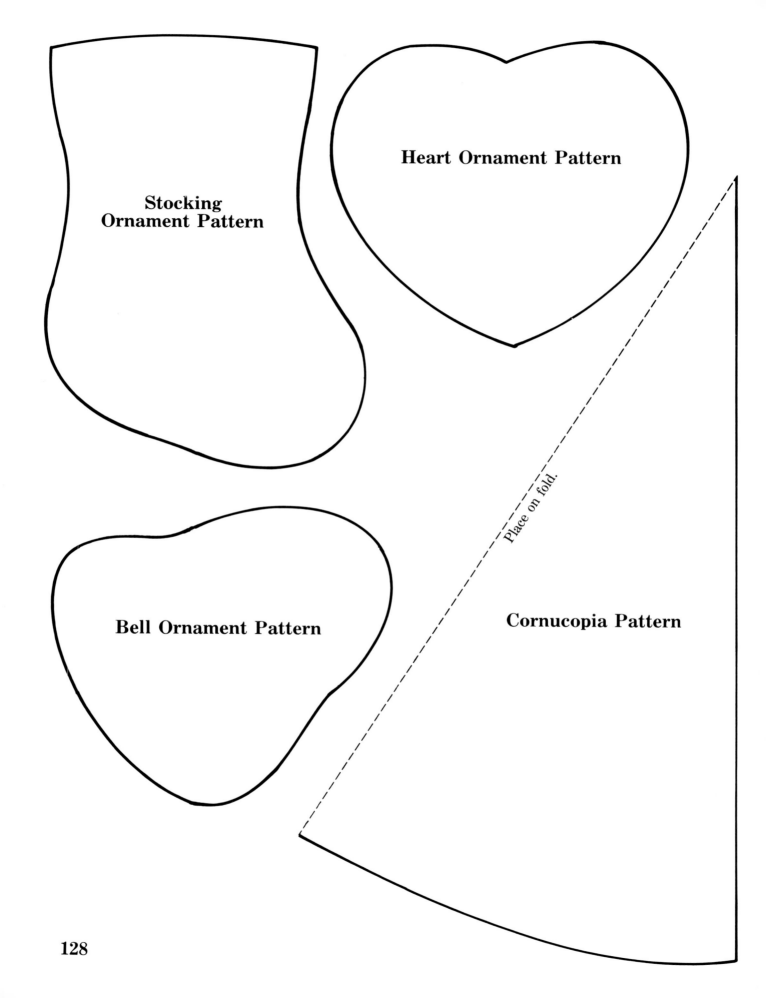

Stocking
Ornament Pattern

Heart Ornament Pattern

Bell Ornament Pattern

Place on fold.

Cornucopia Pattern

128

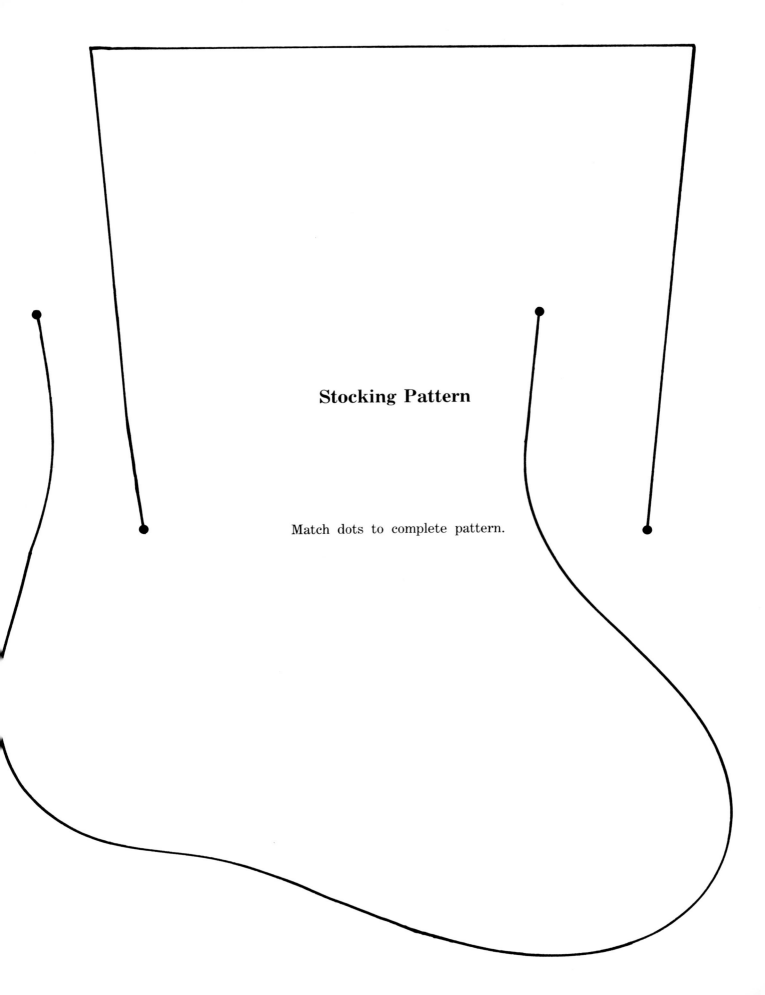

Stocking Pattern

Match dots to complete pattern.

DECEMBER 25
Christmas Day

Special wool stitches create a textured appearance that really brings this old-fashioned Santa to life. His beard looks so soft and fluffy that you'll want to reach out and touch it, and the sleigh, with its three-dimensional effect, looks as if Santa has just stepped out of it after a long night's journey; the stars even twinkle. The needlepoint canvas, scrubbed with a brown wash, adds an antique look.

Santa with Sleigh

SAMPLE
Stitched on Needlepoint Canvas 14 over 1 mesh, the finished design size is 16" x 14⅞". The canvas was cut 22" x 21". Before stitching, thumb-tack canvas to stretcher bars. Make a wash from brown acrylic paint thinned with water to desired consistency. Scrub onto canvas with a rag. Allow to dry thoroughly. See Suppliers for Paternayan Persian yarn and #8 Braid.

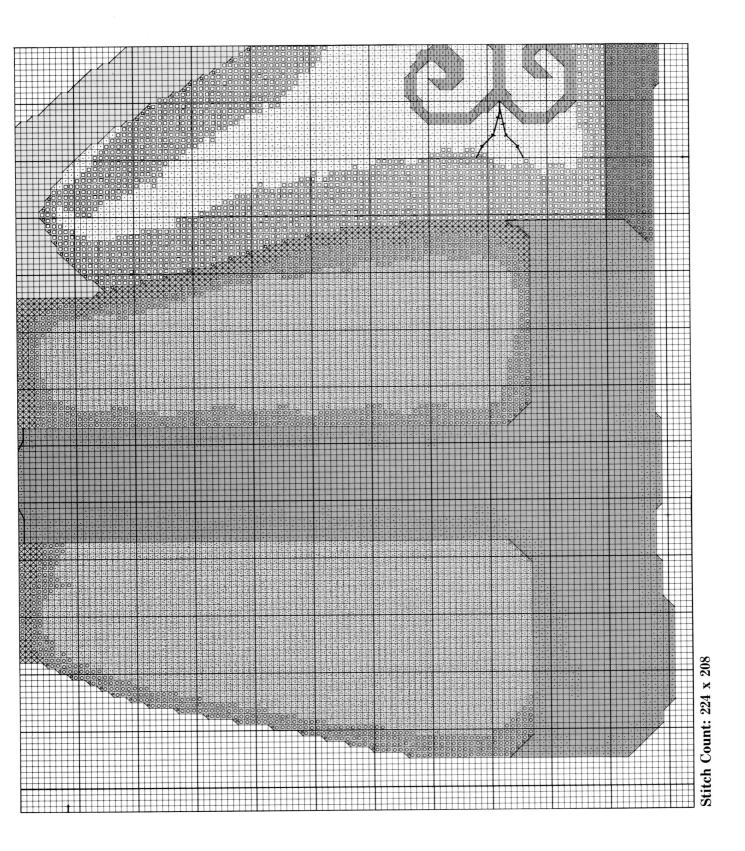

Paternayan Persian Yarn

Step 1: Cross-stitch (2 strands)

	•	261 Cream
	–	875 Rust-vy. lt.
	◁	873 Rust
	∴	950 Strawberry-vy. dk.
	○	940 Cranberry-vy. dk.
	✕	900 American Beauty-vy. dk.
	▮	661 Pine Green-dk.
	□	445 Golden Brown-vy. lt.
	✕	431 Chocolate Brown-dk.
	◉	201 Steel Gray-dk.
	●	220 Charcoal
	∴	032 Pearl Balger #8 Braid (1 strand)

Step 2: Palestrina Knot (1 strand)

	261 Cream
•	445 Golden Brown-vy. lt.

Step 3: Long Stitch (at random) (1 strand)

	261 Cream
	445 Golden Brown-vy. lt.

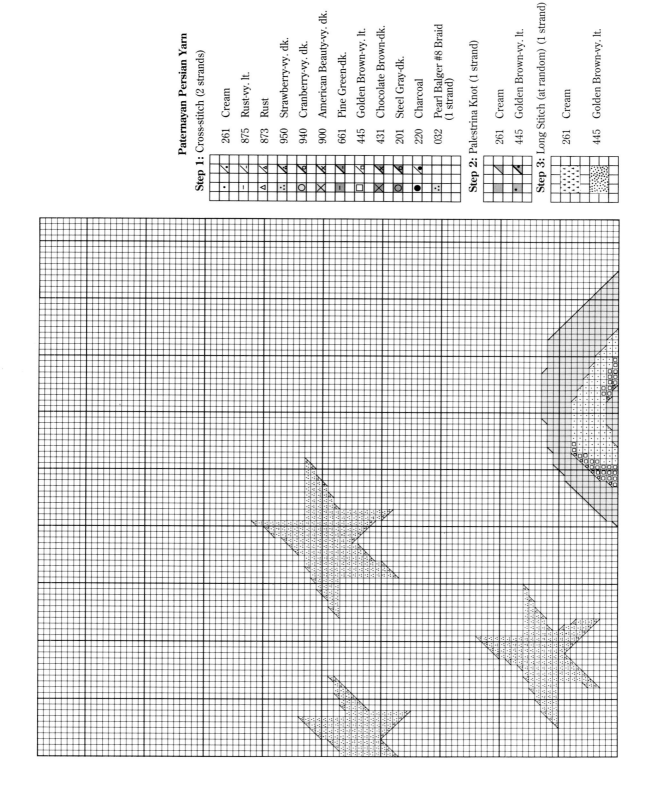

134

Step 4: Satin Stitch (1 strand)

•			

261   Cream
732   Honey Gold-med.

DMC Floss (used for sample)
Step 5: Backstitch (1 strand)

839   Beige Brown-dk.

Paternayan Persian Yarn
Step 6: Couched thread (1 strand)

661   Pine Green-dk.

Step 7: Beadwork

00968   Red

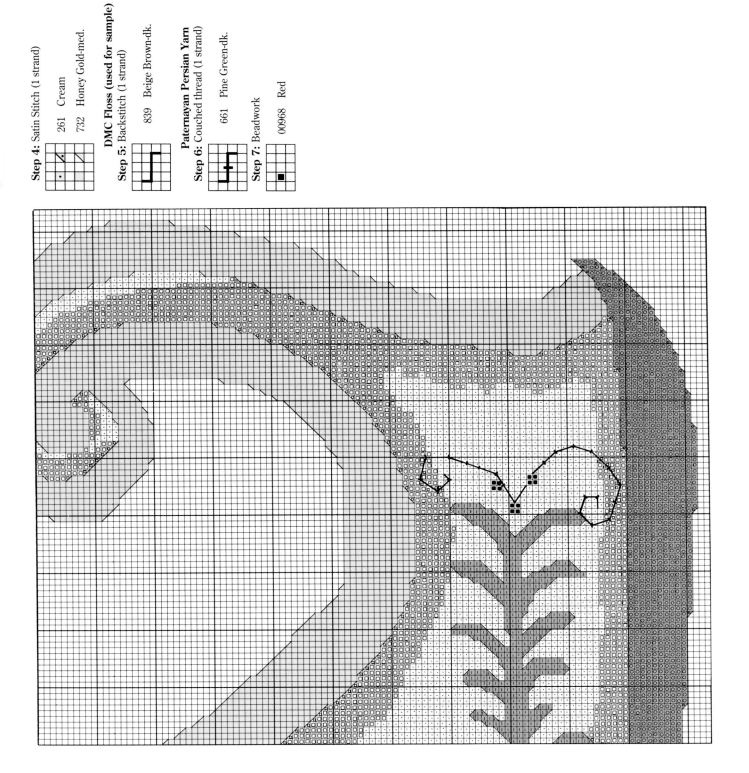

DECEMBER 31
New Year's Eve

This beautifully stitched Scottish proverb is a reminder of the many friends—some old, some new—that each of us has. As we sing the traditional New Year's Eve song from which the words come, we reflect upon these friendships and enjoy the memories associated with them.

Stitch Count: 296 x 115

Should Auld Acquaintance Be Forgot

SAMPLE
Stitched on country Quaker Cloth 28 over 2 threads, the finished design size is 21⅛″ x 8¼″. The fabric was cut 28″ x 15″.

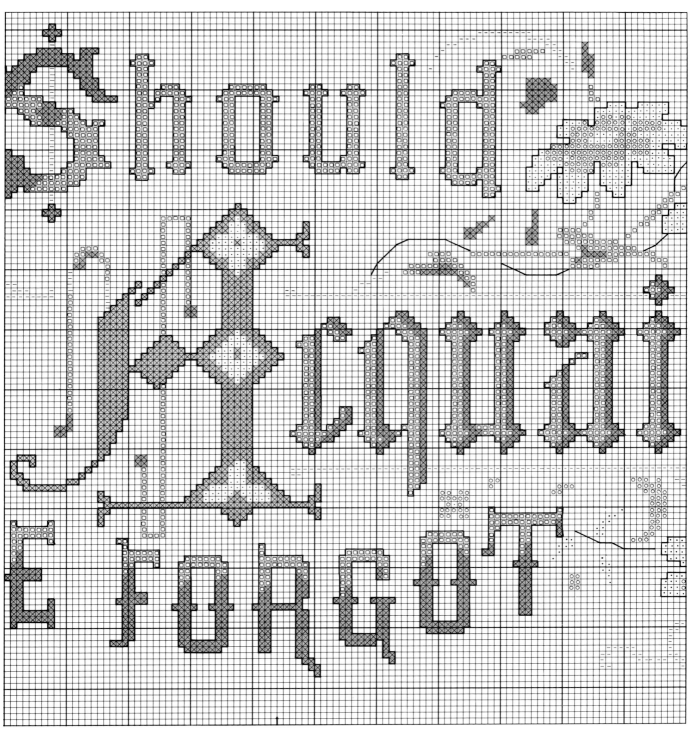

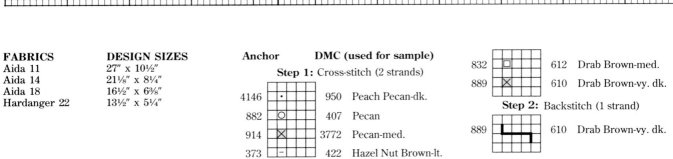

FABRICS
Aida 11
Aida 14
Aida 18
Hardanger 22

DESIGN SIZES
27" x 10½"
21⅛" x 8¼"
16½" x 6⅜"
13½" x 5¼"

Anchor   DMC (used for sample)

Step 1: Cross-stitch (2 strands)

4146	·	950 Peach Pecan-dk.
882	O	407 Pecan
914	X	3772 Pecan-med.
373	−	422 Hazel Nut Brown-lt.
832	□	612 Drab Brown-med.
889	X	610 Drab Brown-vy. dk.

Step 2: Backstitch (1 strand)

889	▬	610 Drab Brown-vy. dk.

General Instructions

Cross-Stitch

Fabrics: Most designs in this book are worked on even-weave fabrics that are made especially for cross-stitch and can be found in your local needlework shop. If you cannot find a particular fabric, see Suppliers for ordering information. Fabrics used in models are identified in sample information by color, name, and thread count per inch.

Preparing Fabric: Cut fabric at least 3″ larger all around than design size or cut it the size specified in sample information. A 3″ margin is the minimum amount of fabric required to insure enough space for matting, framing, and other finishing techniques for stitched piece. To keep fabric from fraying, whipstitch or machine-zigzag along all raw edges, or apply liquid ravel preventer.

Needles: Needles should slip easily through holes but not pierce fabric. For fabric with 11 or fewer threads per inch, use needle size 24; for 14 threads per inch, use needle size 24 or 26; for 18 or more threads per inch, use needle size 26. Never leave needle in design area of fabric. It may leave rust or a permanent impression on fabric.

Hoop or Frame: Select a hoop or stretcher bar frame large enough to hold entire design. Using a hoop or frame keeps fabric taut and makes it easier to make uniform stitches. Place screw or clamp of hoop in a 10 o'clock position (or 2 o'clock, if you are left-handed) to keep it from catching floss.

Centering Design: To find center of fabric, fold it in half from top to bottom and then from left to right. The intersection of folds is center. To find center of design, follow vertical and horizontal arrows until they intersect. Match centers of fabric and design. Begin stitching at this point.

Finished Design Size: To determine size of finished design, divide stitch count by number of threads per inch of fabric. When design is stitched over 2 threads, divide stitch count by half the threads per inch.

Floss: Cut 18″ lengths of floss. For best coverage, separate strands. Dampen with wet sponge. Then put back together number of strands called for in color code.

Securing Floss: Bring needle and most of floss up through fabric, leaving a 1″ tail of floss on underside. Secure loose floss with first few stitches.

Another method for securing floss is the waste knot. Knot floss and insert needle from right side of fabric about 1″ from design area. Work several stitches over thread to secure. Cut off knot.

To secure floss after stitching is completed, run needle under 4 or 5 stitches on back of design and clip tail close to fabric.

Stitching Method: For smooth stitches, use the push-and-pull method. Push needle straight up through fabric, pulling floss completely through to front of fabric. Bring needle to back by pushing needle straight down, pulling needle and floss completely through to back of fabric. Do not pull thread tight. For even stitches, tension should be consistent throughout.

Carrying Floss: To carry floss, weave it under previously worked stitches on back. Do not carry floss across any fabric that is not or will not be stitched. Loose strands, especially dark ones, will show through fabric.

Twisted Floss: Floss covers best when lying flat. If floss begins to twist, drop needle and allow floss to unwind itself. To keep floss from twisting and knotting during stitching, use strands no longer than 18″.

Cleaning Completed Work: When stitching is complete, soak finished piece in cold water with mild soap for 5 to 10 minutes. Rinse thoroughly. Roll work in towel to remove excess water; do not wring. Place work face down on dry towel and, with iron on warm setting, iron until work is dry.

Beadwork

First, attach beads to fabric with diagonal stitch, lower left to upper right. Secure beads by returning floss through beads, lower right to upper left (Diagram A). Complete row of diagonal stitches before returning to secure all beads.

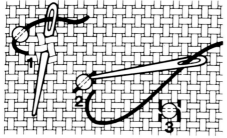

Diagram A

Sewing Hint

Bias Strips: Bias strips are used to make ruffles, binding, or corded piping. To cut bias strips, fold fabric at a 45° angle to grain of fabric and crease. Cut on crease. Cut additional strips the width indicated in instructions and parallel to first cutting line. Ends of bias strips should be on grain of fabric. Place right sides of ends together as shown and stitch with ¼″ seam (Diagram B). Continue to piece strips until they are length indicated in instructions.

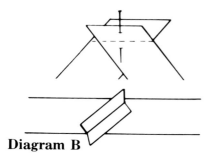

Diagram B

Common Stitches

Cross-stitch: Make 1 cross for each symbol on chart. Bring needle and thread up at A, down at B, up at C, and down again at D (Diagram C). For rows, stitch from left to right and then back (Diagram D). All stitches in row should lie in same direction.

Diagram C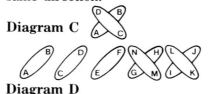

Diagram D

Half-cross: Half-cross is indicated on graph with a slanted line and color symbol beside it. Make longer stitch in direction of slanted line. Stitch actually fills ¾ of area. Bring needle and thread up at A, down at B, up at C, and down at D (Diagram E).

Diagram E

French Knot: Bring needle up at A. Wrap floss around needle 2 times (unless indicated otherwise in instructions). Insert needle beside A, pulling floss until it fits snugly around needle. Pull needle through to back (Diagram F).

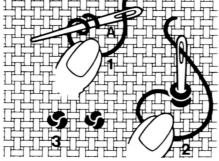

Diagram F

Backstitch: Complete all cross-stitching before working backstitches or other accent stitches. Working from right to left with 1 strand of floss (unless indicated otherwise in color code), bring needle and thread up at A, down at B, and up at C. Going back down at A, continue in this manner (Diagram G).

Diagram G

Plastic Canvas
Stitching on plastic canvas is similar to stitching on fabric; however, graph and color code will look different. Instead of symbols representing yarn or floss colors *inside squares* of grid, on plastic canvas these symbols are printed on *intersections* of grid. Therefore, although the basic motion of cross-stitching will be the same, you will be counting meshes instead of holes. When stitching is complete, carefully cut in space between bar of last row of stitching and next row of unstitched canvas. Then trim nubs left from cutting between bars for a smooth edge. After a design on plastic canvas has been stitched and cut out, the edges are often finished by overcasting with evenly spaced and slanted diagonal stitches (Diagram H). The overcast stitch can also be used to join 2 or more pieces of plastic canvas. Simply align raw edges at angle required to complete project and work stitches to join those edges.

Diagram H   **Overcast Stitch**

Special Stitches

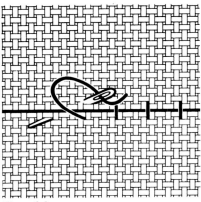

Couching

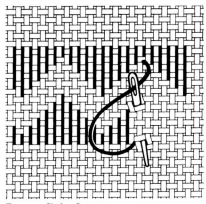

Long Stitch

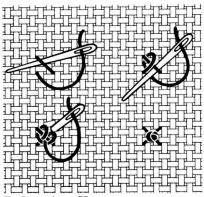

Palestrina Knot

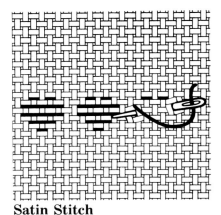

Satin Stitch

Continental Stitch

Suppliers

All products are available retail from Shepherd's Bush, 220 24th Street, Ogden, UT 84401; (801) 399-4546; or for a merchant near you, write the following suppliers:

Zweigart Fabrics—Zweigart/Joan Toggitt Ltd., Weston Canal Plaza, 2 Riverview Drive, Somerset, NJ 08873

Zweigart Fabrics used:
White Aida 14
Black Damask Aida 14
Rustico 14
Needlepoint Canvas 14
Needlepoint Canvas 18
Cream Hardanger 22
Yellow Petit Point Canvas 22
Dirty Linen Dublin Linen 25
Wedgewood Lugano 25
Ivory Linda 27
Khaki Linda 27
Country Quaker Cloth 28
Apricot Pastel Linen 28
Periwinkle Pastel Linen 28
Cracked Wheat Murano 30
Moss Green Murano 30
Cream Belfast Linen 32
Driftwood Belfast Linen 32
White Belfast Linen 32

Natural Aida 14 and Natural Super Linen 27—Charles Craft, P.O. Box 1049, Laurinburg, NC 28352

Yellow Glenshee Linen 29—Anne Powell, P.O. Box 3060, Stuart, FL 34995

Overdyed Floss—Needle Necessities, P.O. Box 8199, 10922 North East 133rd Street, Kirkland, WV 98034

Paternayan Persian Yarn—Johnson Creative Arts Inc., Scales Lane, Townsend, MA 01469

Gold Madeira—Madeira Marketing Limited, 600 East 9th Street, Michigan City, IN 46360

#8 Braid—Kreinik Mfg. Co., Inc., 1708 Gihon Road, Parkersburg, WV 26101

Cream Plastic Canvas 14 and Vanessa-Ann Afghan Weave 18—Chapelle Ltd., P.O. Box 9252, Newgate Station, Ogden, UT 84409

Shaker Table (#47601)—Sudberry House, P.O. Box 895, Old Lyme, CT 06371

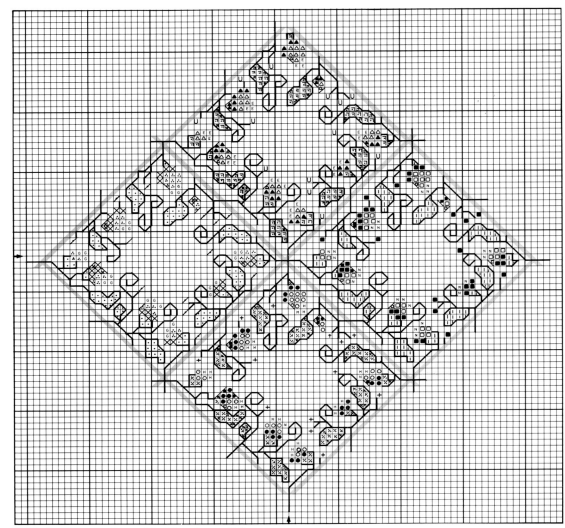

Stitch Count: 84 x 82 (for 1 motif)

Jacket Motif

SAMPLE
Stitched on wedgewood Lugano 25 over 2 threads, the finished design size for 1 motif is 6¾″ x 6½″.

FABRICS	DESIGN SIZES
Aida 11	7⅝″ x 7½″
Aida 14	6″ x 5⅛″
Aida 18	4⅝″ x 4½″
Hardanger 22	3⅞″ x 3¾″

Overdyed Floss (used for sample)

Step 1: Cross-stitch (2 strands)

316	O	◐	740	Tangerine
332	●	◖	946	Burnt Orange-med.
339	+		920	Copper-med.
28	□	◿	3706	Melon-med.
35	■	◢	3705	Melon-dk.
75	△	◺	604	Cranberry-lt.
77	▲	◸	602	Cranberry-med.
66	∴	◹	3688	Mauve-med.
88	✕	◿	718	Plum
98	U		553	Violet-med.
119	╱		333	Blue Violet-dk.
208	·	◿	563	Jade-lt.
187	I	◿	992	Aquamarine
256	◙	◿	704	Chartreuse-bright
266	⊡	◿	3347	Yellow Green-med.

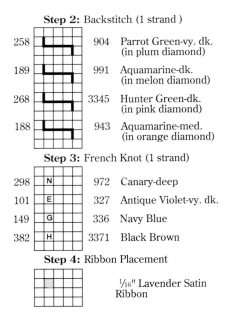

Step 2: Backstitch (1 strand)

258		904	Parrot Green-vy. dk. (in plum diamond)
189		991	Aquamarine-dk. (in melon diamond)
268		3345	Hunter Green-dk. (in pink diamond)
188		943	Aquamarine-med. (in orange diamond)

Step 3: French Knot (1 strand)

298	N	972	Canary-deep
101	E	327	Antique Violet-vy. dk.
149	G	336	Navy Blue
382	H	3371	Black Brown

Step 4: Ribbon Placement

	¹⁄₁₆″ Lavender Satin Ribbon